VOLUME 3   **2023**

HAYMANOT
JOURNAL

SGH MAMHERS (advisory board): Tim Allison,
Vincent Bacote, Vince L. Bantu, Quonekuia Day,
Jacqueline Dyer, Carolyn Palmer, Cleotha Robertson, Nicholas Rowe

**GENERAL KATABIS
VINCE L. BANTU
JACQUELINE T. DYER**

Copyright © 2023 by Vince L. Bantu and Jacqueline Dyer, Editors
www.meachum.org

All rights reserved.
No part of this book may be reproduced or transmitted in any form or by any means, electronic or mechanical, including photocopying, recording, video, or by any information or retrieval system, without prior written permission from the publisher except for the use of brief quotations in a book review.

Published in the United States by Urban Ministries, Inc.
P. O. Box 436987
Chicago, IL 60643
www.urbanministries.com

ISBN 978-1-68353-997-1 (paperback)
ISBN 978-1-68353-998-8 (ebook)

All scripture quotations, unless otherwise indicated, are taken from the NASB, NRSV, NIV, Lexham English Bible (LEB) and Nestle-Aland Greek New Testament (Novum Testamentum Graece) 28th Edition.

Printed in the United States of America

Table of Contents

1. Introduction. 1
   Vince L. Bantu & Jacqueline Dyer

   Sankofa
   Umfundi: Nicholas Rowe

2. "Daughters of the Kisse: The Presence of Foreigners in
   Christian Nubia" 3
   Vince L. Bantu

   Haymanot
   Umfundi: Vincent Bacote

3. "A Biblical-Theological Case for Systemic Sin". 17
   Kenneth J. Reid

4. "Racial Minorities and the Question of Christian Unity" 39
   Gregory W. Lee

5. "These Black Dry Bones Will Live Again: A Pneumatological
   Ideation of the Black Church's Liberation from Social Death" . 50
   Leon Harris

   Ujamaa
   Umfundi: Lori Banfield

6. "Black Marriage as Social Justice". 67
   Preston and Charonda Boone

7. "Developing a Pastoral Response to Racial Trauma" 82
   Melanie Taylor

8. "The Haymanot of the Metaverse". 101
   Michael Schultz

9. "Is There a Word From the Lord? A Black Ecclesial Orthodox
   Theology of Preaching" 117
   Watson Jones III

Book Reviews

"Review of George A Yancey's *Beyond Racial Division: A Unifying Alternative to Colorblindness and Antiracism*" . . . 132
Nicholas Rowe

"Review of Tokunbo R. Adelekan's *8:46 Trumpet of Compassion: George Floyd's Last Breath and the Remaking of America*" . . . 136
Lori E. Banfield

"Review of Love Lazarus Sechrest's *Race & Rhyme: Rereading the New Testament*". 141
Dennis Edwards

"Review of Solange Ashby's *Calling Out to Isis: The Enduring Nubian Presence at Philae*" 145
Mikail Berg

"Review of Vince L. Bantu's *A Multitude of All Peoples: Engaging Ancient Christianity's Global Identity*" 149
Yoknyam Dabale

Introduction

Welcome to the Third Volume of the *Haymanot Journal*

The *Haymanot Journal* publishes the proceedings of the Annual Meeting of the Society of Gospel Haymanot (SGH). SGH is a consortium of Black scholars of biblical, theological, and religious studies that are dedicated to the proclamation of the Bisrat (Gospel) of Jesus Christ, the authority of the Word of Tilli (Old Nubian "God"), the liberation of the marginalized and the embracing of African-descended cultural identity. The theological landscape of academic institutions is characterized, for the most part, by a liberal-conservative binary of which the majority of Black scholars follow the former trend. Meanwhile, the rich tradition of the historical Black Church—one that holds equally to the universal truth of the Bisrat and God's call upon His People for the liberation of the marginalized—is largely absent from graduate institutions of theological education. As daughters and sons of the Black Church and scholars of religious studies, the SGH exists to: 1.) bring the theological perspective of the dominant Black Church—which we call Gospel Haymanot—into conversation with mainstream academia; 2.) create a scholarly community for Gospelist scholars; 3.) reclaim a Black Theology that is grounded in the authority of the Word of God; and 4.) produce Gospelist scholarship that serves the Global Church and institutions of theological education.

The *Haymanot Journal* exists to serve these goals. If one were to search for academic monographs and journal articles on Black Theology or written by Black theologians, they would overwhelmingly represent a theological perspective foreign to the majority of the Black Church. The *Haymanot Journal* exists to provide peer-reviewed scholarship from Black scholars that hold to the Bisrat and to Black liberation. This volume is organized into four disciplines framed by our African forms of knowledge and being: *Dersat* (a Geʽez—classical Ethiopic—term meaning "biblical exegesis"); *Sankofa* (an Akan concept meaning "go back and get it" in the sense of knowing and reclaiming one's history); *Haymanot* (a Geʽez—classical Ethiopic—term meaning "doctrine," "faith," or "theology"); and *Ujamaa* (a Swahili term meaning "collective responsibility" or "family" in the sense of practical ministry and community development). Each paper has been edited by Umfundi (Xhosa terms for "reader") who are discipline specialists, as well as the general Katabis (Geʽez—classical Ethiopic—term for "scribe" or "editor"). Each article was presented at the second Annual Meeting of the SGH, which was held in the fall of 2022. This was our first in-person gathering, coming out of the difficulties of the COVID-19 pandemic. We pray that the scholarship contained in this volume will enrich the academy, support the Church, and glorify the Lord Jesus Christ.

By the grace of Tilli,

Vince L. Bantu
Jacqueline Dyer

Daughters of the Kisse: The Presence of Foreigners in Christian Nubia

Vince L. Bantu

In the capital city Dongola of the central Nubian Kingdom of Makuria, a Christian monastery contains a series of wall paintings from the late-twelfth/early-thirteenth centuries CE. Incorporating Byzantine forms with indigenous Nubian characteristics, the monastery's painting program is unique in both iconography and style. Throughout the monastery, nonbiblical scenes depict figures from potentially different ethnic and cultural backgrounds, which might point to the circulation of sub-Saharan peoples during this period. For example, in the annex of the same Church, a painting of dancers playing distinctive musical instruments abuts a votive image of the Virgin Mary. This painting has raised questions about the potential contact between Christian Nubia and western African neighbors. The following study will examine this painting and place it in the larger context of Nubian contact with other sub-Saharan African cultures. While Nubian contact with Byzantine, Egyptian, and Near Eastern civilizations is well-attested, direct contact between Nubia and western African civilizations is a significantly under-studied area of scholarship. Specifically, this study will examine available evidence for Central and West Africans in Christian Nubia, with the additional goal of understanding their potential contact with Nubian Christianity.

Unlike typical Byzantine depictions of this iconographic type, where the Virgin points to the Child Jesus "as a source of salvation," the Virgin in the Dongola painting gestures toward the scene of the dancers. A vibrant *maphorion chiton* and colorful, voluminous shawls drape the Virgin, who wears a jeweled crown that is "helmet-shaped surmounted by a cross and embellished with a scale motif." The ornate decoration of her attire likely drew from regional inspiration. Abutting the Virgin, Old Nubian inscriptions surround dancers who form three uneven rows. The dancers seem to represent two or three distinct cultures. One group wears sleeveless tunics, pants covered by short skirts, and scarves on their heads and plays percussion instruments. The other group wears short-sleeved tunics, wrapped cloths around their waists, and zoomorphic crest masks while holding a pair of long, cylindrical rods, as seen in the lowest row.

Vincent W.J. van Gerven Oei provides translations of the Old Nubian inscriptions and suggests that the context for the painting was likely Marian's prayers on behalf of the queen mother on the day of the future king's birth.[1] The following is an updated translation of the accompanying inscriptions:

Aaaowa

Aaaowa

The bearer of purity

…king. You are the queen sister for the prince. You are fully the queen sister for him, making one two, queen mother.

Mother Mary, the one who empowers labor

What are you, Mother Mary, what are you? The daughter of the Church, Mother Mary. The Daughter of the Church.

Become pregnant! Cause Mary to become pregnant!

Owow

---

[1] Vincent W.J. van Gerven Oei, "A Dance for a Princess: The Legends on a Painting in Room 5 of the Southwest Annex of the Monastery on Kom H in Dongola," *The Journal of Juristic Papyrology*, 47 (2017): 130.

Owow

Mary takes the mouth…sleep…

I…Mother Mary…[2]

It is of note that the dancers in the first row speak longer, more varied phrases while the dancers who wear masks exclaim onomatopoeias that may have been melodic singing.[3] The Old Nubian inscriptions also raise the question of the potential distinction in religious affiliation between the two groups. While the first group calls on Mother Mary, the second dancer, who makes an unclear, first-person statement, may indicate the invocation of an ancestral deity.[4] It is also significant that the dancers who utter onomatopoeias otherwise unattested in Old Nubian inscriptions also wear animal masks, which are otherwise unattested in Nubian iconography. This suggests that these figures may have spoken a different language than Old Nubian and may have represented traditions from further west in Africa. Martens-Czarnecka associates the African-descended figures with Africans west of the Nubian Nile Valley and offers the Bambara people as a possibility by comparing the images with nineteenth-century evidence from West and Central Africa. Van Gerven Oei claims that the painting "bears witness to a gathering of two different Nubian groups, either constituted as groups for this specific occasion or a reflection of broader social or cultic variety, joining together to perform a ritual that marks an important but also precarious moment in communal life…"[5] Given the uniqueness of elements, such as the animal crest masks, attire, and musical percussion instruments among Old Nubian paintings in a Christian space, it is possible that the second group of

---

[2] This updated translation was done in collaboration with Vincent W.J. van Gerven Oei, and the differences between this translation and his are the result of his own corrections and my own differences in translation.
[3] Vincent W.J. van Gerven Oei, "A Dance for a Princess," 133.
[4] Vincent W.J. van Gerven Oei, "A Dance for a Princess," 134.
[5] Vincent W.J. van Gerven Oei, "A Dance for a Princess," 135.

figures represents a distinct sub-Saharan culture west of the Nubian territory.[6] The importance of the masked figures in this period and this Christian context cannot be overstated. African-art historians have long debated the antiquity of masquerading traditions. This depiction of a masquerade ritual ceremony indicates it was in practice in at least the Dotowan period. While much material and literary evidence from Christian Nubia is likely to be uncovered, there is yet no other example of animal masks in Christian Nubia. Conversely, animal masks are a common feature of many Central, West, and Southern African cultures in the modern world, and they began to appear in West Africa only at least a century after the Dongola painting. Before examining these Dotowan-era masking traditions and their link with Nubia, some preliminary comments on Central and West African links with Nubia are in order.

Christian Nubia most certainly maintained connections with their African neighbors to the west. Indeed, the Nubian language may likely have emerged in the West Kordofan region and then migrated to the Nile River Valley.[7] One of the few discussions on the potential connections between Christian Nubia and West Africa is the suggestion of a link in economic systems between Nubia and the nineteenth-century kingdom of Dahomey. The mid-20th century anthropologist Karl Polanyi argued that Nubia's centralized government and its control of the sale of land and slaves was influenced by a similar model

---

[6] The masks appear to be decorated with cowrie shells, which are used mostly in the Horn of Africa for decorative purposes or as amulets in the medieval period. In his entry about the shells in the *Encyclopaedia Aethiopica*, Wolbert G.C. Smidt notes they were also "used as currency in Ethiopian areas close to the Sudan." In Ethiopia, they are also used as decoration on leather and associated with women, fertility, babies, and milk containers (which can be decorated with giraffe tail hair). Chojnacki notes the Tegrayan Christian annual fertility fest, "which is practiced by women who wish to become pregnant," and peacemaking rituals among some Oromo groups. Interestingly, he notes that cowrie was also used on a first century BCE "golden crown of a Meroitic noble," from Graveyard west, Meroe now at MFA. For cowrie in Ethiopia, see Siegbert Uhlig and Alessandro Bausi, *Encyclopaedia Aethiopica* (Wiesbaden, Germany: Harrassowitz, 2010), 294.

[7] P.L. Shinnie, *Ancient Nubia* (New York, NY: Routledge, 1996), 12.

in Dahomey. However, as pointed out by Giovanni Ruffini, there are several problems with this interpretation. Like the Roman Empire with which Nubia traded, Nubia, in fact, did not have a regulated system of sales imposed by the monarch. Furthermore, there is not much evidence of Dahomey's system of government contemporaneous with Dotowan-era Nubia.[8] Further and perhaps more importantly, there is no extant material or literary evidence demonstrating a connection between Nubia and Dahomey. Rather than simply drawing parallels, this study shall examine evidence demonstrating links between Nubia and Central and West Africa to highlight the plausibility of western foreigners in Nubia. In order to gain an understanding of the presence of western foreigners in Nubia, it is important to explore the extant travel routes that existed between Nubia and Central Africa during the Dotowan period.

By the 10th century, historians such as Ibn Hawqal described defunct caravan routes in Africa that existed at a time when the Sahara was more easily navigable. Ibn Hawqal's report of an interconnected Africa included merchants traveling between Nubia, Egypt, Ethiopia, Ghana, and the Zawila community in the Maghreb:

> The oases in that land was characterized by water, trees, villages and Romans, before the Conquest. From its back part, they traveled to the land of the Sudan and the Maghreb on the road, which they used to travel back in the day from Egypt to Ghana, but it was cut off. This road was not devoid of island palms and a remnant of people. In it to this day there are fruits, sheep and camels, which roam wild in it and hide themselves. The itinerary from Upper Egypt to the frontier of Nubia is about three days in the desert frontier. And their

---

[8] Giovanni R. Ruffini, *Medieval Nubia: A Social and Economic History* (New York, NY: Oxford University Press, 2012), 63–68. Cf. Karl Polanyi, *Primitive, Archaic, and Modern Economies: Essays of Karl Polanyi*, ed. George Dalton (New York, NY: Anchor Books, 1968).

(Nubian) travelers and travelers of the Egyptian people did not proceed on another road; they travelled to the Maghreb and to the land of the Sudan in the wilderness. And this did not stop until the days of Abu al-ʿAbās Ahmad ibn Tulun. They had a road to Fazan and to Barqa, but it discontinued because of what happened to companions in other years, when the winds overwhelmed the companions with sand, to the point that the companions perished. Abu al- ʿAbās ordered that the road be cut off and he stopped anyone from going on it.[9]

Ibn Hawqal's reference to the "back" of the Nile Valley civilizations likely refers to the west and northwestern trade routes across the Sahel. Despite Ibn Hawqal's claims of the Saharan trade routes having faded, later historians closer to the time of the Dongola painting attest to continuing trade between Nubia and their western neighbors. The westward route from Dongola to the neighboring kingdom of Zaghawa was a trodden route by the 14th century:

Ibn Saʾid said: the seat of the Zaghawa is located on longitude 55, latitude 14. Islam is (among) its people and they have accepted the authority of Kanim. The regions where the Zaghawiyyin and the Bajuwiyyin are prominent stretches over the expanse that was upon the bend of the Nile. They are one race (جنس); however, the Bajuwiyyin are better spiritually and physically than the Zaghawiyyin. It says in the ʾAzizi that from Dongola to the land of the Zaghawa is twenty journey phases in the western direction.[10]

Abu al-Fida draws upon the report of Ibn Saʾid but adds the specific duration of time between Dongola and Zaghawa. The account of

---

[9] Ibn Hawqal, *Kitab surat al-ʿArd*, ed. J.H. Kramers (Leiden, Netherlands: Brill, 1938), 153.
[10] Abu al-Fida, *Taqwim al-Buldan*, ed. J.T. Reinaud and W. MacGuckin de Slane (Paris, France: L'Imprimerie Royale, 1840), 159.

Ibn Sa'id also claims that the Daju and the Zaghawa are one "race" (جنس), while also painting the former as morally superior to the latter. Ibn Sa'id's account paints a picture of little interaction between the Nubians and Daju, as well as the Kanembu:

> They (Bajuwiyyin) are infidels (كفار) who are rebels agasint Kanim. They reside in the deserts and mountains of the First and Second Climes. Ibn Fatima recalls that the kings of Kanim and Tajuwa fled with their capitals from the Nile on account of the mosquitoes which are numerous along the flow of the Nile and are thoroughly harmful to men and horses.[11]

Indeed, the 11th-century cartographer Ishaq ibn al-Husayn describes a silent trade between Nubia and the neighboring Zaghawa:

> Gold dust is exchanged for copper there and its people do not understand them (merchants). When a merchant sets out to trade with one of them, he places (what he wants) he places it on the ground. If he is satisfied with it, he takes it. If he is not satisfied with it, he takes his gold and he leaves. And one of their cities is the city of Zaghawa, and it is on the border of the land of the Nuba on the Nile; and the city of Kus and the city of Kawkaw.[12]

Ishaq ibn al-Husayn's report places the Zaghawa between Nubia and the Ghana Kingdom in this gold and copper trade. This report corroborates the connections between Nubia and West Africa. Ishaq also affirms the description of Ibn Sa'id with respect to the limits of communication between Nubia and their immediate neighbors to the west. This may confirm a reading of the Dongola painting, which places onomatopoeias along with the masked figures. Perhaps these masked

---

[11] Ibn Saʻid, *Kitāb basṭ al-arḍ fi-l-ṭūl wa-l-ʻarḍ*, ed. Juan Vernet Gines (Tétouan, 1958), 30.
[12] Ishaq ibn al-Husayn, *Kitāb ākām al-marjān fī dhikr al-madāʼin al-mashhūra fī kull makān* (1988), 104.

figures who don adornment otherwise unattested in Nubian iconography are also representing such western neighbors whose language was largely unintelligible to the majority in Dongola.

Ibn Sa'id also mentions a kingdom called Barkami which was between Nubia, Kanem, and Zaghawa:

> To the north of this moutain range, which stretches from west to east, is the country of the Barkami who are wealthy Sudanese people with valleys between the mountains which have palm trees, water, and vegetation. Those that are next to the country of the Kanim are Muslims, those who are next to the country of Nubia are Christians (نطرئ), and those who are next to the Zaghawa are idolaters (اهل اوثان).[13]

Ibn Sa'id's report of the Barkami is significant in that it reports the spread of Christianity to African kingdoms west of Nubia. If the Barkami lived immediately west of the Nubians and had a Christian population, this would increase the possibilities of trade and travel between these two empires. Indeed, some scholars have identified the name "Barkami" with the Borgu people of modern western Nigeria.[14] Indeed, there are oral histories of the Borgu as well as modern communities in Chad of an ancient people group called the Kisra who migrated across Africa from the Near East. Furthermore, modern members of the Kur'an tribe claim that the ancient ruins at Koro Toro were established by "Black Christians" from prior times. It is also a common

---

[13] Ibn Sa'id, *Kitāb basṭ al-arḍ*, 49. McGregor doubts Ibn Sa'id's report as part of his overall rejection of a Christian presence west of Nubia. In the case of Ibn Sa'id's comments here, McGregor cites Cuoq, who questions the location of the Luniya Mountains. Andrew James McGregor, "The Stone Monuments and Antiquities of the Jebel Marra Region, Darfur, Sudan c. 1000–1750 AD," Ph.D. dissertation (University of Toronto, 2000), 217. Emphasis should be placed, however, on Ibn Sa'id's claim of a distinct people group that is clearly west of Nubia, some of whom are Christian.

[14] N. Levtzion and J.F.P. Hopkins, *Corpus of Early Arabic Sources for West African History*, Third edition (Princeton, NJ: Markus Wiener Publishers, 2000), 445.

assumption among many modern Chadians that ancient material prior to the time of Islam was the result of *Nasara* ("Christians").[15] While this tradition has been doubted by many Western scholars, archaeologists such as Leo Frobenius and H.R. Palmer collected accounts from Central and West African groups of their descent from the Kisra.[16] While there are variations in the account, a Christian figure named Kisra—a person of either Jewish, Miaphysite, or Church of the East background—emerged from Persian or Arabian territory and fled to Egypt. Kisra then lost a battle with the Roman authorities in Egypt and then fled to Nubia, from where his retinue continued to travel west across Africa. While material and literary evidence have not yet been found to corroborate these oral histories, they cannot be entirely dismissed. If it is true that a group of Near Eastern Christians traveled through Egypt, Nubia, and West Africa, this would provide further insight into the presence of foreigners in Nubia. There are literary indications of a group of western foreigners who visited Nubia and who were also Christians. The predecessors of the modern Bilala people of Chad were mentioned by the 12th-century Spanish historian al-Idrisi:

> Sometimes the surrounding area (of Aswan) is invaded by black (السودان) horsemen whose name is the Balbeliyyin, and it is alleged that they are Romans (روم) and have been of the religion of Christianity (دين النصرانية) since the days of the Egyptians, before the emergence of Islam. They are in error, having strayed from Christians. They are Jacobites. They roam about between the land of the Beja and the land of the Habesha, adjoining the land of Nubia. They are men who wander and do not stay in one place, as do the Lamtuna of the desert.[17]

---

[15] McGregor, "The Stone Monuments," 211.
[16] McGregor, "The Stone Monuments," 214–6.
[17] Muhammad al-Idrisi, *Kitab nuzhat al-mushtaq fi ikhtiraq al-afaq,* ed. R. Dozy and M.J. de Goeje (Leiden: Brill, 1866), 22.

While there is no current evidence of the Bilala wearing masks, this narrative by al-Idrisi adds detail to the presence of foreigners in Nubia as well as the spread of Christianity from the Nile Valley further west into Africa. A century after the time of Ibn Sa'id, the 14th-century Amazigh traveler Ibn Battuta described an interconnected Sahel along the Niger River, connecting Dongola with West Africa:

> And then, we set out from Zaghari and we went down the great river, which is the Nile, to the town of Karsachu…and from there, to Kabara…and then to Zagha…and Kabara and Zagha have two sultans who are obedient to the king of Mali. And the people of Zagha are experienced with Islam. They are religious and committed to knowledge. Then the Nile descends from Zagha to Tunbuktu and then to Kawkaw (we shall mention them), then to the town of Muli, a spot which is part of the country of the Limiyyun—which is the last district of Mali—and then to Yufi….which is one of the greatest countries of the Sudan and whose sultan is one of the greatest of their (Sudanese) sultans.[18]

Indeed, the Ife Kingdom that flourished during the 13th to 14th centuries in modern southwestern Nigeria and eastern Benin traded regularly with Nubia as well as Egypt. As early as the second century CE, objects such as mirror stands from Nubia were circulating along the Niger River north of Ife city. During the height of the Ife Empire in the 13th and 14th centuries, Nubian shield rings were discovered in the Ife region.[19] Such Nubian artifacts likely influenced the development of Ife ram images. The Ife also produced some of the earliest-attested masks on the continent of Africa. The most well-known is the

---

[18] Ibn Battutah, *Tuhfat an-nuzzar fi ghara'ib al-amsar wa 'aja'ib al-asfar*, eds. C. Defrémery and B.R. Sanguinetti (Paris, France: L'Imprimerie Nationale, 1879), 395–6. Arabic text. "Yufi" has been identified with modern Ife in Nigeria. J.E.G. Sutton, "Ibn Battuta's Yufi: Bronze and Gold in Mid-Iron-Age Africa," in *Transafrican Journal of History*, 10.1/2 (1981): 160.

[19] Blier, *Art and Risk in Ancient Yoruba: Ife History, Power, and Identity, c. 1300* (New York, NY: Cambridge University Press, 2015), 334.

naturalistic copper mask of King Obalufon II, dated to the early 14th century. Copper was a significant commodity in the Trans-Saharan trade, which connected Nubia, Egypt, and West African civilizations. The Muslim king of Mali, Mansa Musa, described his copper reserves thusly: "There is nothing in all my empire which is such a large source of taxes as the import of this unworked copper. It comes from this mine and from no other. We send it to the land of the black pagans where we sell mithkal of it for 2/3 of gold."[20] It is worth noting that the Mali kingdom to the northwest of Ife also is attested to practice the bearing of masks for ceremonial purposes. In his 14th-century report on the imperial court of Mali, Ibn Battuta reported:

> All of them are inside a form made of feathers like a peeping bird with a wooden head placed on it and a red beak, like the head of a peeping bird. They proceed in front of the sultan in this ridiculous get-up (الهيئة المضحكة) and they recite their poems. I was reminded that their poetry is a form of preaching, in which they say to the sultan: "This *bembi* upon which you sit is that which such-and-such king was upon and were the noble deeds of one and such-and-such were the deeds of another. As for you, do good deeds whose memory will be beyond you."[21]

Despite Ibn Battuta's condescending attitude toward West African civilizations, his report of the existence of masks is significant. The presence of masks is attested through literary and material evidence in various West African contexts during the late Middle Ages. It is noteworthy that no mention of such ceremonial masks has yet been discovered from Nubia during this time period outside of the Dongola painting. One millennium before the flourishing of the Ife Empire, the Nok culture developed extensive iron technology and art in the area of Central Nigeria.

---

[20] Blier, *Art and Risk*, 281.
[21] Ibn Battuta, *Tuhfat an-nuzzar*, 413–414.

Between the third century BCE and the third century CE, the Nok created a wide variety of humanoid terra-cotta figurines that retained exaggerated features with some zoomorphic representations. While there are no extant face masks developed by the Nok, the similarities between the facial constructions on Nok sculptures and modern Yoruba face masks have been noted.[22] It is likely that the Ife masks attested during the 14th century were influenced by Nok artistic conventions. Furthermore, the iron industry that developed in Nok was autochthonous and not the result of foreign influence. However, similar iron-working sites have been found in Carthage, Kush, and Central Africa. Therefore, it is likely that Nok iron smelting developed in contact with surrounding African civilizations. Therefore, Nigerian civilizations participated in trade across the continent during the Axumite and Dotowan periods of African history. The influence of mask-making would have circulated throughout this trade in West Africa and across the Sahel.

The trade that existed between Nubia and West Africa is clearly attested by the existence of Nubian artifacts and artistic conventions. What is even more significant for the purposes of this study is that various Ife artifacts bear cross-shaped incisions that have been identified as a Nubian and Egyptian influence. Pendants, as well as figures, bear cross shapes as well as garments that were influenced by Egyptian and Nubian textile conventions.[23] Oral traditions in Nigeria, as collected by the archeologists Leo Frobenius and J.M. Ita, corroborate the existence of a trade between the Ife and an unidentified Christian group:

> Frobenius collected an account from the Nupe, who claimed that they had learned brass-casting from the people of Issa, or Jesus, who came from a city of white buildings with red (tile) roofs and bronze doors. Frobenius conjectured that they meant the then-Constantinople, forgetting that Alexandria lay

---

[22] Jane Bingham, *African Art & Culture* (Chicago, IL: Raintree, 2005), 18.
[23] Blier, *Art and Risk*, 153, 161, 174.

between. While it is popular these days to discount much of Frobenius' field data, Ita, checking on unpublished data of the former, finds that we would do well to reexamine it in the light of new finds that verify many of the accounts given him by Yoruba informants. The cross appears in both Nupe and Bini bronzes, but today its origin is lost in a confusion of explanations that vary from individual to individual.[24]

Literary evidence and oral traditions indicate that Dotowan-era Nubia was engaged in trade with Central and West African civilizations. It is possible that the masks depicted in Dongola may have been a result of this trade. An Islamic text from a slightly earlier period provides generalized commentary on the practices of sub-Saharan—or "Sudanese"—people groups and makes specific mention of masking customs. The text—*Akhbar al-zaman*—begins by recounting the "Curse of Ham" myth common to Dotowan-era Islamic scholars. The text claims that the "accursed" descendants of Kan'an (Canaan) developed into many "Sudanese" people groups throughout the Maghreb and the Zanj regions. The text claims that the "Sudanese" have a variety of customs, yet highlights certain common characteristics that include masking customs: "Among them are races (اجناس) who clothe themselves in skins and they are naked; and there are others of them who put on grass and there are those among them who make horns of animal bones on their heads."[25] The text continues describing masking traditions in matrimonial contexts:

> When one of them gets married, they smear his face with something similar to ink, and they seat him on a hill and they sit on a hill. And they seat the woman next to him and they make

---

[24] Justine M. Cordwell, "Human Imponderables in the Study of African Art," in *The Visual Arts: Plastic and Graphic*, ed. Justine M. Cordwell, (The Hague, Netherlands: De Gruyter Mouton, 1979), 473.
[25] Pseudo-al-Mas'udi, *Akhbar al-zaman* (Al-Haydariyya Library: Najaf, Iraq, 1977), 87.

something like a cupola with reeds. They stand around it for three days drinking alcohol with maize and turning up. Then they leave and the groom takes his bride and they set out for their resting place. They dress with copper rings in their hands and in the ears of their women. Red-dyed ribbons are brought to them to wear, but no one dresses with them except for the king.[26]

The *Akhbar al-zaman* immediately shifts focus to discussing the customs of the Kawkaw and Ghana kingdoms. This indicates the probability that the aforementioned comments were in reference to these West African civilizations.

In sum, the strongest indication of Nubian connection with Central and Western African communities is in the literary evidence during the Dotowan-era Trans-Saharan trade. Admittedly, material evidence indicating the presence of foreigners in Dongola or other regions of Nubia is lacking. Nonetheless, the presence of northern and eastern neighbors—Romans, Egyptians, Arabs, and Blemmyes—is well attested in literary sources. Yet, these trans-local migrants have also not left a significant material footprint. In the same way, it is evident that Nubians traded extensively with Central and West African neighbors during the Dotowan period. The Dongola painting depicts visual elements otherwise unattested in Nubian iconography. Furthermore, the depiction of Africans wearing animal masks otherwise only appears among the Ife in modern Nigeria and close to the same time period as the Dongola painting. Considering that animal masks are otherwise unattested in Nubia, that animal masks appeared in West Africa during this time period, and that Nubia was connected to West Africa through trade routes, it is most likely that these painting motifs represent traditions that Nubians came into contact with from the west.

---

[26] Pseudo-al-Mas'udi, *Akhbar al-zaman*, **88**.

A Biblical-Theological Case for Systemic Sin

Kenneth J. Reid

Introduction

The purpose of this paper is to broaden the conversation beyond systemic racism to the reality of systemic or structural sin. If sin only can only be committed by individuals without a structural or systemic dimension, then the systemic sin—including racism, sexism, etc.—would lack a biblical foundation; furthermore, theologians and pastors would neglect these social issues as an important aspect of God's renewal purposes for humanity and creation. However, if sin has a systemic dimension, then pastors and theologians are called and obligated to address it academically and in the church. If sin has a systemic or structural dimension, the theologians are called to understand this and to provide answers that God has shown in his word. The urgency of this matter is great because if systemic sin exists, then it leads to many injustices. This article will argue that Scripture provides evidence for systemic sin. Furthermore, the theologies of sin and God provide a basis for the existence of systemic sin. A vibrant ecclesiology can combat systemic sin in the church and provide grounding for dealing with it in the world.

Toward a Definition of Systemic Sin

One challenge regarding a discussion of systemic sin is one of definition. This type of sin is not merely one person committing an act that has corporate effects, such as the sin of Achan.[27] Systemic or structural sin involves many different people or groups of people. It is the interconnected work of people that results in sins that affect individuals and groups.[28]

Many evangelical theological approaches rightly emphasize sin as a product of individual acts or dispositions. Two systematic theologies that are representative of many evangelical definitions of sin are those by Wayne Grudem and Robert Letham. Grudem defines sin as "any failure to conform to the moral law of God in act, attitude, or nature."[29] Letham states that "sin is any transgression of the law of God and thus is directed principally against God."[30] Grudem's and Letham's definitions are broad enough to include the social dimension of sin, but their chapters emphasize the nature of individual sins.

Some evangelical theologians have described systemic or structural sin in their theology of sin. Robert Pyne deals with the collective sin of groups by describing how groups of people commit the seven deadly sins.[31] Millard Erickson devotes an entire chapter of his systematic theology to the social dynamic of sin.[32] In the book *Fallen*, John W. Mahony, in his chapter "A Theology of Sin for Today," devotes a

---

[27] Josh. 7:1–26.
[28] For the purposes of this paper, the terms "structural sin" and "systemic sin" are used interchangeably. Both terms are considered aspects of the social dimension of sin. The social dimension of sin may include structural or systemic sin, as well as the sins committed by an individual with social or corporate effects.
[29] Wayne A. Grudem, *Systematic Theology, Second Edition: An Introduction to Biblical Doctrine*, Second edition (Grand Rapids, MI: Zondervan Academic, 2020), 619.
[30] Robert Letham, *Systematic Theology* (Wheaton, IL: Crossway, 2019), 366.
[31] Robert Pyne, *Humanity and Sin* (Nashville, TN: Thomas Nelson, 1999), 224–44.
[32] Millard J. Erickson, *Christian Theology*, Third edition (Grand Rapids, MI: Baker Academic, 2013), 584–99.

brief discussion regarding how sin is both personal and social.[33] He observes that "social sin is also reflected in the societal structures that propagate the evils of prejudice, hate, and bigotry."[34] One of the most extensive treatments of systemic sin comes from Thomas McCall. He helpfully discusses the contributions of liberation theologians as he deals with structural sin.[35] Perhaps the most comprehensive definition comes from Robert Pyne. He notes that "Anytime we affiliate with people who share our particular purposes, we tend to join them in forwarding and defending those purposes. Any prejudices or sins that are common to the group will be reinforced, not challenged, and any values that are foreign to it are likely to be rejected."[36] He continues:

> The values of a community are often expressed in particular social structures. On a national level our retail and healthcare industries demonstrate our collective commitment to consumerism and vitality, while our educational and political systems reveal our desire for training and order. Such social structures reflect our collective interests, sometimes even enforcing those interests against other nations or groups. That observation raises the possibility that the structures themselves express the collective sin of our community. Many theologians have described this pattern as "structural sin" implying that the prejudices of a particular group live on in the social systems they have created.[37]

---

[33] John W. Mahony, "A Theology of Sin for Today," in *Fallen: A Theology of Sin*, eds. Christopher W. Morgan and Robert A. Peterson (Wheaton, IL: Crossway, 2013), 195–96.
[34] Mahony, "A Theology of Sin for Today," 195.
[35] Thomas H. McCall, *Against God and Nature: The Doctrine of Sin* (Wheaton, IL: Crossway, 2019), 258–70. I am indebted to this section of McCall's book for the resources that he has provided.
[36] Pyne, *Humanity and Sin*, 223.
[37] Pyne, *Humanity and Sin*, 223.

Cornelius Plantinga's definition of sin describes the nature of sin in the context of God's goals for creation. Plantinga describes sin in light of God's shalom. Shalom means *"universal flourishing, wholeness, and delight*—a rich state of affairs in which natural needs are satisfied and natural gifts fruitfully employed."[38] Shalom represents creation without the corrupting effects of sin, and it reflects God's intended design for creation. In light of shalom, Plantinga shares his complete definition of sin:

> But once we possess the concept of shalom, we are in a position to specify our understanding of sin. God is, after all, not arbitrarily offended. God hates sin not just because it violates his law but, more substantively, because it violates shalom, because it breaks the peace, because it interferes with the way things are supposed to be. (In fact, that is why God has laws against a good deal of sin.) God is enthusiastically for shalom and *therefore* against sin. Let's say that evil is any spoiling of shalom, whether physically (by cancer, say), morally, spiritually, or otherwise. Moral and spiritual evil are agential evil, that is, evil that, roughly speaking, only persons can or do have: agential evil thus comprises evil acts and dispositions. Sin is, then, any agential evil for which some person (or group of persons) is to blame. In short, sin is culpable shalom-breaking.[39]

This definition of sin certainly expands the theology of sin to include both the individual and systemic/structural dimensions. Plantinga's definition is helpful because it focuses on God's creational purpose of shalom and how sin undermines that purpose.

---

[38] Cornelius Plantinga Jr., *Not the Way It's Supposed to Be: A Breviary of Sin* (Grand Rapids, MI: Eerdmans, 1996), 10.
[39] Cornelius Plantinga Jr., *Not the Way*, 13–14.

Liberation theologians emphasize the theme of liberation from the perspective of the oppressed. This oppression is experienced through communities of marginalized people. Theologian José Ignacio González Faus observes that "when human beings sin, they create structures of sin, which, in turn, make human beings sin."[40] Reflecting on this dynamic of social sin, Faus cites Óscar Romero's second pastoral letter to present a cogent definition of structural sin as "the crystallization of individual egoisms in permanent structures which maintain this sin and exert its power over the great majorities."[41] From his Latin American context, Faus also reflects on the realities of social sin and that the denial of structural sin would present a negative view of God's character:

> In the Christian notion of sin there are other features besides the fact that sin is the fruit of a personal and responsible freedom. Sin also means that which God rejects and cannot accept in any way. Therefore denying the notion of structural sin is equivalent to saying that the present situation of the world (and in particular the third-world countries) is not a situation that arouses God's rejection and anger. Accepting the notion of structural sin means we are saying that the relationship of all humanity with God has been degraded, precisely because of the degradation in the relationships of human beings to one another.[42]

As a representative of Black Liberation Theology, Frederick Ware presents a helpful description of sin. He states that individual acts of sin must be accounted for in light of the social acts that are oppressive

---

[40] José Ignacio González Faus, "Sin," in *Systematic Theology: Perspectives from Liberation Theology*, eds. Jon Sobrino and Ignacio Ellacuria (Maryknoll, NY: Orbis Books, 1996), 198.
[41] Faus, "Sin," 199. This pastoral letter was composed in 1977.
[42] Faus, "Sin," 199.

to certain groups.[43] He adds, "African American theologians contend that the matter of sin cannot be limited to a discussion or corrective of personal conduct. Sin must be dealt with in its social manifestation. Since sin is manifested socially, it needs to be addressed in a social manner."[44]

Thus, the working definition of systemic or structural sin is that expressed by a group of people, which reflects their collective values—thus, the systems and structures they have created perpetuate the prejudices within the created social system and their policies.[45] While it will involve many personal sins, the systemic nature of it rises beyond personal sins to the way that organizations, through policies and culture, perpetuate the mistreatment of others. Systemic sin opposes God's creational purpose of shalom.

Biblical Evidence

Though some evangelicals and many liberation theologians have discussed systemic sin, they usually have limited the discussion to contemporary issues of sexism, racism, and poverty. While this is important, the discussion would have some stronger grounding if systemic sin could be grounded biblically. This section examines biblical support for systemic sin.

The Bible itself does not have a term for structural/systemic sin, but systemic sin is present in Scripture. How does one recognize when systemic sin is present in Scripture? I propose two criteria to discern structural sin. First, the biblical description of the specific sin is not

---

[43] Frederick L. Ware, *African American Theology: An Introduction* (Louisville, KY: Westminster John Knox Press, 2016), 142.
[44] Ware, *African American Theology*, 142. Bruce Fields observes, "Black theology as a movement reminds the church of the pervasiveness of sin in systems, structures, and sociopolitical institutions. Systemic sin should be thought of as the bentness of human nature manifested in the perpetuation of injustice to, and dehumanization of, select groups in sociocultural constructs," Bruce L. Fields, *Introducing Black Theology: Three Crucial Questions for the Evangelical Church* (Eugene, OR: Wipf & Stock Publishers, 2019), 66–67.
[45] Pyne, *Humanity and Sin*, 223.

limited to an individual but possesses a social dynamic. Many people participate in this act or support it—sin does not arise from only one person—which results in communal consequences.[46] Second, God expresses his disapproval in response to this sin. These two criteria should reveal the presence of systemic sin in Scripture.

The first example of structural sin is the enslavement of the Israelites in Egypt. Exodus 1:8–22 explains the Egyptians' hearts, fears, and rationale for enslavement. This new king, who did not know Joseph,[47] instituted a program of population control out of fear that the Israelites would outnumber the Egyptians and form alliances with their enemies.[48] The Egyptians, under the leadership of Pharaoh, enslaved the Israelites and imposed hard labor on them.[49] When the Israelites continued to grow in population, Pharoah unsuccessfully ordered the Hebrew midwives to kill all the infant males once they are born.[50] Eventually, Pharaoh gives the order to kill all the Hebrew male infants.[51]

Several factors indicate that this is an example of systemic sin. The enslavement of the Israelites involved many people. Pharaoh established laws and policies as a part of his government program to enslave the Israelites and to execute the Hebrew infant boys. He explained his reasons through government propaganda, presenting a narrative of population control to enforce national security (with a hint of racial superiority). Egyptian society approved and participated in the oppression. Douglas Stuart notes:

> Moses' wording of this verse [verse 11] implies that the pharaoh's proposal was accepted and its implementation begun fairly rapidly—at least rapidly enough that Moses felt no need

---

[46] Though this is one dimension of the social aspect of sin.
[47] Ex. 1:8
[48] Ex. 1:9–10
[49] Ex. 1:11–14
[50] Ex. 1:15–21
[51] Ex. 1:22

to describe any intervening developments between the proposal and its implementation. It obviously was an incremental policy of population control designed to suppress gradually the Israelites' will and ability to resist.[52]

Later in Exodus, Moses notes God's disapproval of this treatment by remembering the Israelites,[53] and he judged the Egyptians for their acts of slavery and infanticide.[54] These factors indicate that Egyptian enslavement of the Israelites was an act of systemic sin.

The presence of systemic sin is present in the prophetic writings in Scripture. God made a covenant with Israel, the Mosaic covenant, that he would be their God and they would be his people. God's requirement is that his people, the Israelites, would worship and serve him and they would follow his laws. His laws included ceremonial and sacrificial acts of worship and the standard by which individuals and nations would live together. Several scriptures point to the presence of injustice, the need to repent, and God's concern for the poor and the marginalized.[55] Amos 5:10–18 provides an example of systemic sin.

Amos is an 8th century BC prophet to the Southern Kingdom of Judah. One of his themes is injustice in Judah, which he addresses in Amos 5:10–18. Among the issues that he addresses to the Southern Kingdom are injustice in court and those who lie in court,[56] those who impose taxes on poor people so that they may enrich themselves,[57] and their oppression of the innocent and taking bribes that deprive the poor of justice in court.[58] The nature of the sins indicates that this is a part of the political and social order in Israel. Making unjust laws,

---

[52] Douglas K. Stuart, *Exodus: An Exegetical and Theological Exposition of Holy Scripture* (Nashville, TN: B&H Publishing Group, 2006), 66.
[53] Ex. 2:23–25
[54] Ex. 6:1–8
[55] See Isaiah 1:10–17, 10:1–3, and Micah 6:8 as examples.
[56] Am. 5:10
[57] Am. 5:11
[58] Am. 5:12–13

oppressive decrees, and oppression by government law and enforced by others suggests a systemic dimension of injustice in their society. Gary Smith notes:

> Justice is an outworking of God's character of holiness, but the nation does not emulate him. They have changed the sweet experience of dealing with people based on righteousness into a bitter and evil thing though their mistreatment of those who are poorer or less powerful. By manipulating the courts through bribery, supplying false witnesses, and intimidating judges, the powerful political and business leaders are able to maintain their lifestyles and insulate themselves from accusations of unfairness. Amos laments these unbearable injustices. These rich people make life miserable for the poor, who suffer under them.[59]

The systemic nature of their actions is clear in this passage. God disapproves and expresses it through the prophetic words of Amos. Furthermore, God's conviction against the nation of Israel for various injustices has been expressed in the prophetic passages:

> Woe to those who make unjust laws, to those who issue oppressive decrees, to deprive the poor of their rights and withhold justice from the oppressed of my people, making widows their prey and robbing the fatherless. What will you do on the day of reckoning, when disaster comes from afar? To whom will you run for help? Where will you leave your riches? (Isa 10:1–3)

> This is what the Lord says: "For three sins of Israel, even for four, I will not relent. They sell the innocent for silver, and the needy for a pair of sandals. They trample on the heads

---

[59] Gary V. Smith, *The NIV Application Commentary: Hosea, Amos, Micah* (Grand Rapids, MI: Zondervan Academic, 2001), 314–15.

of the poor as on the dust of the ground and deny justice to the oppressed. Father and son use the same girl and so profane my holy name. They lie down beside every altar on garments taken in pledge. In the house of their god they drink wine taken as fines. (Amos 2:6–8)

These constitute systemic sin. Overall, Robert Pyne summarizes the presence of systemic sin as the prophets have addressed it:

Such devastation cannot be explained simply by appealing to the sinful actions of their leaders. The kings and patriarchs did sin, and their individual decisions did have corporate consequences, but the communities themselves had also collectively rebelled against God. They established their own power through the violent oppression of other peoples (Amos 1:3, 6, 9, 11, 13). They rejected the Law of God and pursued other deities ([Amos] 2:4; Jer. 10:1–25). They oppressed the poor (Amos 2:6–7; 4:11 5:12) while living extravagantly in luxurious homes (6:4–7). They demonstrated arrogance in the belief that their cities were secure and invulnerable (6:1–3; Jer. 48:42; Obad 1:3). Their public officials demanded bribes and their personal friends betrayed confidences (Mic. 7:3; 5–6). They refused prophetic correction while pursuing their own lusts, believing they would surely escape judgment (Jer. 5:7–13). They were sinful individuals who compounded their guilt through sinful communities.[60]

One New Testament passage that may exhibit a case for systemic sin is James 2:1–13. James rebukes the church for showing partiality. He notes that those who are rich (have good clothes and a gold ring) are given special favor over the person who is poor (has filthy old clothes).[61]

---

[60] Pyne, *Humanity and Sin*, 222–23.
[61] Jas. 2:1–4

While James addresses the corporate body of the church in these areas, this seems to indicate that this problem is not just isolated to one group of people; this is characteristic of the community. At best, this favoritism for the wealthy, as a cultural distinctive of Roman society, is characteristic of a portion of the community or, at worst, the entire community.[62] If this is part of the culture of the church, with leaders and the people involved, this seems to have a systemic dimension. This letter of correction indicates that James—and God, who inspired this letter—does not approve of these actions. McCartney notes that "discriminatory seating is of a piece with the perversion of justice that all too frequently occurs in secular courts, and thus it is an implicit denial of faith in the God who shows no partiality."[63] The act of favoritism to the rich may constitute systemic sin for the church that James addresses.

Believers are commanded not to love the world or anything in the world.[64] Loving the world and loving God the Father are mutually exclusive.[65] The world contains the "lust of the flesh, the lust of the eyes, and the pride of life," which do not come from the Father.[66] Jesus also instructs that the since the world hates him, it will hate his followers because they have been chosen out of the world.[67] D. A. Carson notes that "the world, as commonly in John, refers to the created moral order in active rebellion against God."[68] The world is not just a collection of isolated individuals. It is the collective of individuals, systems, and even cosmic forces arrayed against Jesus and his followers. The world in John's theology is a system. The destructive patterns of the world occur both individually and especially systemically. The

---

[62] David P. Nystrom, *The NIV Application Commentary: James* (Grand Rapids, MI: Zondervan Academic, 1997), 117.
[63] Dan G. McCartney, *James* (Ada, MI: Baker Academic, 2009), 140.
[64] 1 Jn. 2:15a
[65] 1 Jn. 2:15b
[66] 1 Jn. 2:16
[67] Jn. 15:18–19
[68] D. A. Carson, *The Gospel According to John*, Reprint edition (Grand Rapids, MI: Eerdmans, 1991), 525. See pages 122–23 for an extended discussion of the term "world" in John's Gospel.

world as a system shows the reality of systemic sin. Erickson explains the systemic and evil nature of the world:

> The world as a whole organized system of spiritual force is a fact. It is the very embodiment of evil. It is a pervasive entity that exists quite apart from particular evil individuals; it is the structure of all reality apart from God. It is a mindset and frame of reference totally different from and opposed to that of Christ and his disciples.[69]

Revelation focuses on corporate sin in the beginning of the book. The church in Ephesus is held to account because it had forsaken its first love;[70] the church in Thyatira tolerates a false prophet[71] who leads them into sexual immorality; the church in Sardis is dead;[72] and the church at Laodicea is lukewarm because they are independent and rich, being blind to their condition. Each of these churches committed some type of communal sin. The Lord, through his messages from the angel, invites them to repent and promises a reward. While individuals have a role in sin and repentance, the focus of the message is the church.[73]

The Bible provides evidence for systemic sin. Egyptian slavery of the Israelites displeases God and is an act of the Egyptian government and society. The sins of Israel's leaders in the treatment of their citizens bring forth God's call to repent and are a violation of their covenantal obligations. The world system is sinful, and sinful acts are carried out throughout this system. The favoritism in the churches possibly demonstrates the structural nature of sin. God's message to the churches in Revelation points to systemic sin within the congregations.

---

[69] Erickson, *Christian Theology*, 590.
[70] Rev. 2:4
[71] Rev. 2:20
[72] Rev. 3:1
[73] Werner Mischke, "Sin is complex: it is cosmic, collective, individual," 2021. Culture Learner. https://wernermischke.org/tag/systemic-sin/ (accessed February 1, 2023).

Theological Evidence

This section focuses on the theological evidence for systemic sin. It begins with an argument that critical areas in the theology of sin support systemic sin. This section also examines how the attributes of God's righteousness and justice to the nations support the presence of structural sin. Finally, God's creation of the church and his plan for the church is an answer to the presence of structural sin.

Theology of Sin

A theology of systemic/structural sin is a fundamental component of a vibrant theology of sin. It is grounded on original sin, the universality of sin, and total depravity. The following is a brief summary of these theologies to show how they support systemic/structural sin.

Paul states that all people have sinned and fall short of God's glory.[74] He argues that all people, those without the law and those under the law, are accountable before God and are, by nature, corrupt.[75] Paul continues to explain that people are united with Adam in their sin, as well as united with Christ in their redemption.[76] The theology that follows from Romans 5:12–21 is called original sin. Original sin is the doctrine that connects the sin of every person to Adam. Bird notes that "original sin has been used in the Western church to describe the inherited corruption and collective guilt that humanity received from Adam."[77] He adds, "The heuristic value of the doctrine of original sin is first, that it explains the universal and inevitable nature of sin. Second, that sin belongs to the nature of human beings in their fallen

---

[74] Rom. 3:23
[75] Rom. 3:9–18
[76] Rom. 5:12–21
[77] Michael F. Bird, *Evangelical Theology, Second Edition: A Biblical and Systematic Introduction*, Second edition (Grand Rapids, MI: Zondervan Academic, 2020), 777.

state."⁷⁸ This doctrine shows that it belongs to humanity after the fall; it is inherited from our ancestors and traced to Adam.⁷⁹

Because all people have inherited sin, all people possess a corrupted nature that grounds their behavior, attitudes, and disposition (without Christ)—the doctrine of total depravity does not mean that every person commits evil at their highest capacity. Instead, it points to the holistic corruption of each person and, by implication, of humanity. All people are corrupted, but it is total in three ways. First, it is total "in the broadly extensive sense that it impacts all members of the human race."⁸⁰ In a second sense, it is total because it affects the whole person. Michael Horton states that "what is meant by 'total' is that the whole nature of humanity, not only the body and its desires but the soul, mind, heart, and will, is corrupt."⁸¹ The third way that it is total is that it is expressed in all the acts and attitudes that unredeemed humanity commits.⁸² Thus, all people are corrupted in their will, intellect, bodies, hearts, and in every constitution of the human person. As such, the acts that follow from each person are corrupted.

Original sin and total depravity ground systemic sin. Original sin means every human being bears corruption and guilt. Each human being is totally depraved in the sense that each person is corrupted in all aspects of the human constitution. Both original sin and total depravity point to the universality of sin, that corruption is in every human being. Thus, the actions of humanity

---

[78] Bird, *Evangelical Theology, Second Edition*, 777.
[79] Michael F. Bird, *Evangelical Theology: A Biblical and Systematic Introduction* (Grand Rapids, MI: Zondervan, 2013), 677. In his first edition, Bird also states that "our disobedience has a historical beginning and a material cause in the disobedience of Adam." For various views of original sin, see McCall, *Against God and Nature*, 153–202. I agree with Erickson that a person is not held guilty of their sin until they can make a conscious decision to sin. See Erickson, *Christian Theology*, 528.
[80] McCall, *Against God and Nature*, 309.
[81] Michael Horton, *The Christian Faith: A Systematic Theology for Pilgrims on the Way* (Grand Rapids, MI: Zondervan Academic, 2011), 433.
[82] McCall, *Against God and Nature*, 310.

reflect this corruption, then it follows that the systems or structures formed by Adam's descendants reflect this corruption. Faus states that "when human beings sin, they create structures of sin, which, in turn, make human beings sin."[83] Though every person may not sin in the system, the actions that they take and contributions to the system, if the system is flawed and motivated and marked by sin, the system will result in sinful actions that display the corruption of the people who created the system. Furthermore, Dr. Martin Luther King, Jr. notes that the evils that are present in society create an atmosphere in which people who would never commit such evils (racism, misogyny) individually are encouraged to sin within groups in order to gain social approval.[84] Governments, laws, and organizations will show the sinful effects as they operate. One potential objection is that one must be culpable of sin, and corporate entities are not culpable. However, God holds nations and groups of people culpable of sin. If sin is a spoiler of shalom, as noted by Plantinga, and if the racism, greed, sexism, and exploitation that occurs through collective action is a violation of God's shalom, this follows that this collective action is sin.

God's Attributes of Righteousness and Justice

Two of God's attributes are righteousness and justice. God's righteousness means that "the law of God, being a true expression of his nature, is as perfect as he is."[85] Erickson continues, stating that "the righteousness of God also means that his actions are in accord with the law he himself has established. He is the expression in action of what he requires of others."[86] God, as a God of justice,

---

[83] Faus, "Sin," 198.
[84] Dr. Martin Luther King, Jr., "Man's Sin and God's Grace," Stanford University: The Martin Luther King, Jr. Research Education Institute. https://kinginstitute.stanford.edu/king-papers/documents/mans-sin-and-gods-grace (accessed February 2, 2023).
[85] Erickson, *Christian Theology*, 258.
[86] Erickson, *Christian Theology*, 258.

administers justice, and he holds humanity accountable for their actions. Erickson states: "God's justice means that he administers his law fairly, not showing favoritism or partiality." [87] As one who upholds justice in his own actions, God requires it of others. Thomas Oden observes:

> The biblical ground for insisting upon fair dealings between people is that God, being righteous, requires righteousness (Amos 5:24; Mic. 6:8; Ps. 15:1–2). God, as One wholly just, requires justice in human relationships. Especially those who are called and authorized to exercise public justice and mete out judgment in human affairs are to be placed beside the plumb-line of divine justice (Amos 7:7, 8).[88]

Why judge nations and corporate entities? God clearly judges Israel and the other nations around Israel.[89] God's judgment points to a collective element in their sin—their sin is not merely an individual phenomenon but one that the whole society commits.

Ecclesiology

One response to systemic sin, particularly in the church, is shown in God's design and purpose for the church. This section will focus on the mission of the church, the unity and holiness of the church, and the church as a community of fellowship.

The Mission of the Church

The mission is to spread the Gospel to all nations and to build up the body of Christ. Does the Church have a mission to the world

---

[87] Erickson, *Christian Theology*, 259.
[88] Thomas C. Oden, *Systematic Theology, Vol. 1: The Living God* (Peabody, MA: Hendrickson Publishers, 2006), 105.
[89] Is. 13–22

and society at large? Absolutely! The Church has a duty to be a witness to the world and to represent righteousness. The practices of righteousness as a witness to the world include caring for the poor and marginalized.[90] The Apostles urged Paul to remember the poor,[91] and the Church has ministered to the world in concrete acts of feeding the hungry, setting up orphanages, and caring for widows. The Church has always regarded its mission to the world as broader than evangelism. The Church has also addressed societal problems in its local context. One important example is the work of African American churches. Many churches have advocated for freedom and equality in the public square. A part of their ministry has been to address systemic sin in the forms of slavery, disenfranchisement, lynching, and economic injustice. African American churches expect their pastors to address the practical issues, such as fair wages, the treatment of children and women at work, and the unjust economic system.[92] Benjamin Mays and Joseph Nicholson observed:

> When the Negro pastor feels the urge to preach a thoroughgoing gospel of brotherhood, applying it to the Negroes, whites, Japanese, Chinese, and other races, it is gladly received by Negro audiences. It is taken for granted that Negro ministers will courageously oppose lynching, Jim Crow law, and discrimination in the expenditure of tax money, especially as applied to schools, parks, playgrounds, hospitals, and the like.[93]

---

[90] Gregg R. Allison, *Sojourners and Strangers: The Doctrine of the Church* (Wheaton, IL: Crossway, 2012), 462.
[91] Gal. 2:10
[92] Benjamin E. Mays and Joseph W. Nicholson, "The Genius of the Negro Church," in *African American Religious History: A Documentary Witness*, Second Edition, ed. Milton C. Sernett (Durham, NC: Duke University Press, 1999), 433–34.
[93] Mays and Nicholson, "The Genius of the Negro Church," 434.

These comments reflect the way African American churches preached in their congregations, which resulted in their ministry efforts in American society. Yet the Church has never been insular and only focused on evangelism. The early Church dealt with the issues in their society. They cared for the poor, and they rescued babies who were abandoned to exposure and death.[94] The mission of the Church has always been broader than evangelism and ministry inside the Church. Thus, the Church has regularly addressed, either through proclamation or acts of justice, the systemic sins in the surrounding society.

Unity and Holiness of the Church

In the Nicene-Constantinopolitan Creed (381 AD), the ancient marks of the Church are summarized in one sentence: "We believe in one, holy, catholic, and apostolic church." For the purposes of this article, I will focus on the unity and holiness of the Church. Jesus prayed that his Church would be one,[95] and the unity of the Church is a vital mark from its beginning. Paul uses the body metaphor in relation to both the local church[96] and the universal Church[97] to best exemplify the unity of the Church. The Church is one body and many members (local and universal church); if one part is harmed, then the whole body suffers. In one sense, unity is accomplished because the Spirit unites each believer into the Church through his baptism,[98] and God

---

[94] For this practice and the critiques against it, see Tertullian, "The Apology," in *Ante-Nicene Fathers: Volume 3*, eds. Alexander Roberts, James Donaldson, Philip Schaff, and Henry Wace (Peabody, MA: Hendrickson, 2004), 24–26; Tertullian, "Ad Nationes," in *Ante-Nicene Fathers: Volume 3*, eds. Alexander Roberts, James Donaldson, Philip Schaff, and Henry Wace (Peabody, MA: Hendrickson, 2004), 123–24.
[95] Jn. 17:20–21
[96] 1 Cor. 12
[97] Eph. 2
[98] 1 Cor. 12:13

has provided the gift of oneness.[99] Yet we are commanded to maintain the unity that God has provided for us. Therefore, "affirming the unity of the church means affirming that the church, which is endowed with oneness, pursues the end of perfect unity by working diligently to maintain its unity."[100] At a minimum, we should be engaging in practices that heal or lift up the whole body. Systemic sin harms a part of the body of Christ. Early 20th-century African American pastor Francis Grimké described the segregation practices that undermine this unity of the Church. He observed that predominantly white churches in the southern states rejected the African American as a member and did not allow them to attend in a separate space in the church. Churches in the northern states were no better, as African Americans were still not welcomed:[101] "The simple fact is, when they venture, occasionally, into these churches, they are not treated with the same courtesy, with the same cordiality as white people are treated."[102]

A second quality of the Church is holiness. The Church is holy as a people who have been set apart for God's purposes. But God's church is called to practice holiness in its actions.[103] Bird adds: "Holiness is central to the church's mission. If the distinction between the church and the world is lost, the church forfeits its right to speak for God, and its members risk coming under God's judgment."[104] The presence of structural sin, especially in the church, is antithetical to God's vision of the holiness of the church.

---

[99] Allison, *Sojourners and Strangers*, 168.
[100] Allison, *Sojourners and Strangers*, 168.
[101] Francis J. Grimké, "Christianity and Race Prejudice (June 5, 1910)" in *The Faithful Preacher: Recapturing the Vision of Three Pioneering African-American Pastors*, ed. Thabiti M. Anyabwile (Wheaton, IL: Crossway, 2007) 136–137.
[102] Grimké, "Christianity and Race Prejudice," 137.
[103] "Holiness is both a God-given status and an ethical state for the church to live up to. Holiness is created by God's consecration of the church for himself. Yet God also calls his people to live in holiness before him." Bird, *Evangelical Theology, Second Edition*, 834.
[104] Bird, *Evangelical Theology, Second Edition*, 835.

The Church Is a Community of Fellowship

God created the church as a fellowship community. In the early church, the design of the church is expressed in Acts:

> They devoted themselves to the apostles' teaching and to fellowship, to the breaking of bread and to prayer. Everyone was filled with awe at the many wonders and signs performed by the apostles. All the believers were together and had everything in common. They sold property and possessions to give to anyone who had need. Every day they continued to meet together in the temple courts. They broke bread in their homes and ate together with glad and sincere hearts, praising God and enjoying the favor of all the people. And the Lord added to their number daily those who were being saved.[105]

The Church is the community for a profound type of fellowship. They shared all things in common, devoted themselves to the apostles' teaching, prayed, and ate together. They shared life together. At this early point, we see the Church unified, practicing holiness, devoted to apostolic preaching, and gathered. Though these qualities fluctuate as the Church matures, Acts 2:42–47 displays God's desire for his Church through its fellowship. Tragically, systemic sin undermines God's design, especially when it occurs in the Church. Howard Thurman reflects on the American Church and the manner in which systemic sin has destroyed unity and fellowship:

> American Christianity has betrayed the religion of Jesus almost beyond redemption. Churches have been established for the underprivileged, for the weak, for the poor, on the theory they prefer to be among themselves. Churches have

---

[105] Acts 2:42–47

been established for the Chinese, the Japanese, the Korean, the Mexican, the Filipino, the Italian, and the Negro, with the same theory in mind. The result is that in the one place in which normal, free contacts might be most naturally established—in which the relations of the individual to his God should take priority over conditions of class, race, power, status, wealth, or the like—this place is one of the chief instruments for guaranteeing barriers.[106]

Conclusion

This study has presented a biblical-theological case for systemic sin. Systemic sin is the sin as expressed by a group of people, which reflects their collective values—thus, the systems and structures they have created, be it organizations or nations, perpetuate the prejudices within the social system and their policies.[107] Systemic sin is found in Scripture. It is seen in the Egyptian enslavement of the Israelites and in the acts of Israel's leaders and people who the prophets revealed as they asked Israel to repent. The world as a system commits systemic sin, and New Testament passages about favoritism and the messages to the churches in Asia Minor in Revelation display some examples of structural sin. The theology of original sin and total depravity sets the foundation for the existence of systemic sin. God's judgment of nations points to the presence of structural sin. God's design for the Church in its mission—its essence as a unified and holy church—is incongruent with systemic sin in the church and in the surrounding culture.

What is at stake? Our mission as a church. Our mission as witnesses of Jesus Christ is important. Jesus cared for the needs of the people on the ground. The Gospel is good news certainly for the

---

[106] Howard Thurman, *Jesus and the Disinherited*, Reprint edition (Boston, MA: Beacon Press, 1996), 98.
[107] Pyne, *Humanity and Sin*, 223.

salvation of humanity. However, Jesus did not separate the spiritual needs and everyday physical needs of people. God calls us to love our neighbors as ourselves. Dealing with systemic sin in our churches and society is a concrete avenue to love our neighbors. The contradiction of the effort to save souls for heaven while neglecting justice or, at worst, participating in injustice undermines the Church's mission.[108]

---

[108] Howard Thurman, *The Luminous Darkness*, First edition (Richmond, IN: Friends United Press, 2014), 63–65.

Racial Minorities and the Question of Christian Unity

Gregory W. Lee

Since the 1920s Fundamentalist-Modernist Controversy, white American Protestants have been divided between "conservatives" who espouse traditional doctrines but eschew social justice and "liberals" who valorize social justice but disregard traditional doctrines. Racial minorities who embrace both sets of concerns often find themselves ecclesially and institutionally homeless, especially when they belong to white, especially evangelical, communities that dismiss the significance of race.

This challenge has intensified following the 2016 presidential election. Though scholars have studied evangelicalism and race for some time, the issue has received widespread attention through recent publications like Jemar Tisby's *The Color of Compromise*, Robert Jones's *White Too Long*, and Anthea Butler's *White Evangelical Racism*, each of which presents racism as a central theme in evangelicalism's history.[109] A disturbing number of white evangelicals—including

---

[109] Jemar Tisby, *The Color of Compromise: The Truth about the American Church's Complicity in Racism* (Grand Rapids, MI: Zondervan, 2020); Robert P. Jones, *White Too Long: The Legacy of White Supremacy in American Christianity* (New York, NY: Simon & Schuster, 2020); Anthea Butler, *White Evangelical Racism: The Politics of Morality in America* (Chapel Hill, NC: University of North Carolina Press, 2021). A related discussion concerns evangelicalism's failures concerning gender. See Kristin Kobes Du Mez, *Jesus and John Wayne: How White Evangelicals Corrupted a Faith and Fractured a Nation* (New York, NY: Liveright, 2020); Beth Allison Barr, *The Making of Biblical Womanhood: How the Subjugation of Women Became Gospel Truth* (Grand Rapids, MI: Brazos, 2021); Amy Peeler, *Women and the Gender of God* (Grand Rapids, MI: Eerdmans, 2022). For discussion, see ed. Mark

celebrated figures in evangelical history—owned slaves, supported Jim Crow, resisted or remained silent during the Civil Rights Movement, rejected residential and school integration, and opposed interracial dating at Christian colleges and seminaries.[110] There is intellectual and genealogical continuity between those who opposed racial justice in previous eras and those who do so now.

At the same time, scholars have increasingly noticed minority Protestant communities characterized by traditional *theology* and progressive *social positions*. These communities challenge the binary between white (theological and political) liberals and white (theological and political) conservatives. Mary Beth Swetnam Mathews's *Doctrine and Race* has found that Black Protestants during the Fundamentalist-Modernist Controversy generally sided with the fundamentalists on doctrine and with the modernists on justice, affirming the virgin birth as they decried fundamentalist racism and affirming the "brotherhood of man" as they decried modernist departures from the Bible.[111] Daniel Bare's *Black Fundamentalists* has identified Black Protestants during this time who actually called themselves fundamentalists.[112]

These studies align with contemporary works by minority authors espousing traditional theology and progressive social interests, at least to a certain degree. Representative texts include Esau McCaulley's *Reading While Black*, Christina Edmondson and Chad Brennan's *Faithful Antiracism*, Robert Chao Romero's *Brown Church*, Sandra Maria Van Opstal's *The Next Worship*, Randy Woodley's *Indigenous*

Labberton, *Still Evangelical?: Insiders Reconsider Political, Social, and Theological Meaning* (Downers Grove, IL: IVP Books, 2018).

[110] This history has been acknowledged by prominent evangelical leaders. See Timothy Keller, "The Decline and Renewal of the American Church: Part 2 — The Decline of Evangelicalism," Winter 2022. *Life in the Gospel*. https://quarterly.gospelinlife.com/the-decline-of-evangelicalism (accessed December 9, 2022).

[111] Mary Beth Swetnam Mathews, *Doctrine and Race: African American Evangelicals and Fundamentalism between the Wars* (Tuscaloosa, AL: The University of Alabama Press, 2017).

[112] Daniel R. Bare, *Black Fundamentalists: Conservative Christianity and Racial Identity in the Segregation Era* (New York, NY: New York University Press, 2021).

Theology and the Western Worldview, and Daniel Lee's *Doing Asian American Theology*, all of which promote theology resonant with the social contexts of their respective communities.[113] There are also several institutional ventures. Among African Americans, examples include The Witness, The Jude 3 Project, and (of course) Meachum School of Haymanot. Among Latinos/as, there are World Outspoken, Fuller Theological Seminary's Centro Latino, and the Brown Church initiative. Native Americans have Indigenous Pathways, NAIITS: An Indigenous Learning Community, and iEmergence. From Asian Americans, we can add Fuller Theological Seminary's Center for Asian American Theology and Ministry, Princeton Theological Seminary's Center for Asian American Christianity, and the Asian American Christian Collaborative.

These initiatives raise complicated questions concerning Christian unity. According to some conservative Christians, discourse about race is inherently divisive because it concentrates our attention on what distinguishes us as opposed to what unites us, namely, Jesus Christ. Race is a political issue and not a Gospel matter. Different opinions about race do not justify rupturing the unity to which Christ has called us. Minorities who critique or withdraw from a white Christian community because of its alleged failures on race divide the body of Christ and prioritize secondary, debatable issues over the essentials of Christian faith. Thus, race- or ethnic-specific Christian groups like the ones I have mentioned have tenuous grounds for existing. By

---

[113] Esau McCaulley, *Reading While Black: African American Biblical Interpretation as an Exercise in Hope* (Downers Grove, IL: IVP Academic, 2020); Christina Edmondson and Chad Brennan's *Faithful Antiracism: Moving Past Talk to Systemic Change* (Downers Grove, IL: IVP, 2022); Robert Chao Romero, *Brown Church: Five Centuries of Latina/o Social Justice, Theology, and Identity* (Downers Grove, IL: IVP Academic, 2020); Sandra Maria Van Opstal, *The Next Worship: Glorifying God in a Diverse World* (Downers Grove, IL: IVP Books, 2015); Randy S. Woodley, *Indigenous Theology and the Western Worldview: A Decolonized Approach to Christian Doctrine* (Grand Rapids, MI: Baker Academic, 2022); Daniel D. Lee, *Doing Asian American Theology: A Contextual Framework for Faith and Practice* (Downers Grove, IL: IVP Academic, 2022).

establishing contexts independent from white Christians, they risk the sin of separatism.

In general, adherents of this perspective affirm the legitimacy of division under certain circumstances, especially in response to severe violations of doctrine or morality. They simply do not believe various forms of racial oppression constitute severe violations of faith. I disagree with this perspective and would like to offer two reasons why. Both these reasons are social and historical in character. Neither has received much attention in traditional discussions of church unity. They thus suggest the inadequacy of reflection on church unity that is theoretical alone.

Race and Doctrine

First, racial division between Christians does not derive from disagreement on traditional doctrines. As Jason Shelton and Michael Emerson have observed, there is virtually no difference between white and Black Protestant Americans in their affirmations that God exists, God created the world, Jesus Christ was divine, Jesus physically rose from the dead, and heaven and hell exist.[114] Robert Putnam and David Campbell report the same in *American Grace*. In comparison to evangelical Protestants, Black Protestants are more likely to say that Scripture should be taken literally, the world will end soon, and the world was created in the last 10,000 years.[115] They are also more likely to read the Bible daily, attend church every week, say that religion is important for their personal decisions, and describe religion as an important part of their identity. Black Protestants match or exceed white evangelicals in doctrinal conservatism and religious activity.

---

[114] Jason E. Shelton and Michael O. Emerson, *Blacks and Whites in Christian America: How Racial Discrimination Shapes Religious Convictions* (New York, NY: New York University Press, 2012), 50–53 and 216–18.

[115] Robert D. Putnam and David E. Campbell, *American Grace: How Religion Divides and Unites Us* (New York, NY: Simon & Schuster, 2012), 274–84.

This phenomenon is not restricted to comparisons between Black and white Christians. As has been much discussed, 80% of white evangelicals voted for Donald Trump in the 2016 election. To speak of my own demographic, that number for Asian American evangelicals was 37%.[116] There is a twofold *political* difference between white and Asian American evangelicals that has nothing to do with *theological* differences. Indeed, as American Studies professor Janelle Wong has found, except for abortion and homosexuality, Asian American evangelicals are considerably more liberal than white evangelicals on virtually every political issue. This population constitutes the strong majority of Asian American Protestants. Among students of Asian descent enrolled in Association of Theological Schools (ATS) institutions, nearly 70% attend a Protestant evangelical school—which is not even to count Asian and Asian American students in mainline institutions who are evangelical in their beliefs.[117] Yet Asian American evangelicals do not fit the binary between white liberals and white conservatives. We affirm traditional theological doctrines, but we are not beholden to conservative politics.

During the 1980s, at the invitation of the National Council of Churches and the World Council of Churches, a group of Black theologians, pastors, and laypersons investigated the relation between Black Christianity and the ecumenical movement.[118] In a later reflection on these discussions, Gayraud Wilmore observed, "African American Christians, for the most part, have never taken for granted that the Apostolic Faith, being invoked by the World Council of Churches, is resident in the white churches of Europe and North America—Protestant

---

[116] Janelle S. Wong, *Immigrants, Evangelicals, and Politics in an Era of Demographic Change* (New York, NY: Russell Sage Foundation, 2018), 21.

[117] Daniel O. Aleshire, *Beyond Profession: The Next Future of Theological Education* (Grand Rapids, MI: Eerdmans, 2021), 67.

[118] Gayraud S. Wilmore, "Black Christians, Church Unity, and One Common Expression of Apostolic Faith," in *Pragmatic Spirituality: The Christian Faith through an Africentric Lens* (New York, NY: New York University Press, 2004), 247–48.

or Roman Catholic [...] mere assent to the Nicene Creed and adherence to the great confessions of the Reformation do not, by themselves, add up to apostolicity."[119] As he clarifies, Black Christians have affirmed the Apostles' and Nicene Creeds in their official statements of faith,[120] and they have resisted mainline denominations' tendency to accommodate Christian faith to the Enlightenment.[121] Yet Black churches reject the division between religion and politics that white Christians have deployed to avoid issues of racial justice. And some have questioned whether any church that practiced or defended slavery could be considered Christian without total repentance and reform.[122] "It is not unfair to ask whether at some time during the last millennium the message of Jesus Christ and the New Testament all but evaporated from the Euro-American churches and societies because of the gross incompatibility between faith and practice in race relations among those who called themselves Christians."[123]

The differences between white and minority churches challenge traditionalist approaches to church unity. It does not suffice to establish a set of doctrinal or ethical positions as the basis for Christian unity and to dismiss other reasons for separation as divisive—at least not when these positions are defined by white Western Christians whose racial failings are the reason minorities have developed alternate communities in the first place.

---

[119] Wilmore, "Black Christians, Church Unity, and One Common Expression of Apostolic Faith," 250.

[120] Wilmore, "Black Christians, Church Unity, and One Common Expression of Apostolic Faith," 251.

[121] "Their African American denominational counterparts, while they, too, came to stress the importance of an educated ministry, were never so sanguine as the white brethren about theological seminaries, demythologizing the Bible, or making systematic and moral theology subservient to secular philosophies and ethics." Wilmore, "Black Christians, Church Unity, and One Common Expression of Apostolic Faith," 254.

[122] Wilmore, "Black Christians, Church Unity, and One Common Expression of Apostolic Faith," 250.

[123] Wilmore, "Black Christians, Church Unity, and One Common Expression of Apostolic Faith," 250.

In the early 1900s, the *National Baptist Union-Review* asked how fundamentalist preachers like Billy Sunday could "denounce adultery, fornication, liars, hypocrites, bums, hobos, rascals, scoundrels, crap shooters, tramps and loafers, and leave untouched the lynchers, the ballot box thief, the segregator, the discriminator, the Negro hater, the promotor of racial strife and the mob leader who burns human beings at the stake because they are black."[124] Similar questions apply today. Do certain beliefs or practices concerning race constitute severe violations of doctrine or morality? Is racial justice always off the table when it comes to the primary issues of Christian faith? Which populations set the terms for this discussion? What legitimizes predominantly white institutions dictating the boundaries of discourse about race? These are questions that traditional ecclesiologies have generally not pursued.

Race and Place

The failure of traditional theology in this area relates to our second concern, namely, the social and historical realities of place. Church division is a function of geographical division. These divisions are so pervasive that we often take them for granted. Few metropolitans embody them more starkly than my own city, Chicago. As an exercise for our urban programs at Wheaton College, we require students to ride the L from one end to another and to observe the demographic composition of the passengers as the train proceeds through different neighborhoods. Almost any line will do: the Red Line, the Green Line, the Pink Line, and so forth. Our students immediately perceive the disparities, which signal unmistakably which areas are white, Black, or Latino/a, which areas are higher income, lower income, or somewhere in-between. They also observe the disparities between Chicago and its suburbs, many of which are overwhelmingly white and wealthy.

---

[124] Mathews, *Doctrine and Race*, 143.

These divisions are a social and ecclesial scandal. Residential boundaries dictate property value, the quality of schools, access to public transportation, access to food, economic opportunities, crime rates, indicators of public health, and other social metrics.[125] Churches reflect these divisions, as Christians typically worship with those of the same demographic within the geographies that have been designated for them. Churches of different socioeconomic statuses have different material concerns with vastly unequal resources to serve their own communities.

Residential and ecclesial divisions embody a history of racial injustice. Chicagoland divisions between white and Black populations began in the early 1900s when millions of African Americans migrated north to pursue industrial jobs and to escape the terrorism of Jim Crow. This story has been recounted many times in both academic and popular-level works by Isabel Wilkerson, Beryl Satter, William Julius Wilson, Ta-Nehisi Coates, and others. What has received less attention is how white *Christians* responded to the migration, namely, by also resisting integration and moving to the suburbs.

Consider the examples of Englewood and Roseland, two low-income African American neighborhoods in Chicago's South Side. Englewood is the neighborhood Spike Lee featured in his movie *Chi-Raq*, which suggested that certain parts of Chicago are war zones. Roseland is the neighborhood where Obama worked as a community organizer for three years. These neighborhoods were once the epicenter of the city's Dutch Reformed population. The Christian Reformed

---

[125] Douglas S. Massey and Nancy A. Denton, *American Apartheid: Segregation and the Making of the Underclass* (Cambridge, MA: Harvard University Press, 1993); Patrick Sharkey, *Stuck in Place: Urban Neighborhoods and the End of Progress toward Racial Equality* (Chicago, IL: The University of Chicago Press, 2013); Richard Rothstein, *The Color of Law: A Forgotten History of How Our Government Segregated America* (New York, NY: Liveright, 2017). For an accessible Christian treatment of this matter, see David Leong, *Race and Place: How Urban Geography Shapes the Journey to Reconciliation* (Downers Grove, IL: IVP Books, 2017).

Church first entered Englewood and Roseland in the mid-1800s.[126] By 1900, the greater Chicago area was second only to Grand Rapids, Michigan, for the greatest number of Dutch persons in this country, with a strong Dutch culture that discouraged interaction with Catholic, Jewish, non-Christian, or even Christian-but-not-CRC communities.[127] The dominant vehicles of neighborhood life were the CRC church and the CRC school, which tended to compete with opportunities for social and political engagement and were easily moveable in the event of demographic change.[128]

African Americans began moving into these neighborhoods in the 1940s. Though much of the Black population was Protestant, it was met with immediate hostility and occasional violence by the Dutch Reformed community.[129] As sociologist Mark Mulder has detailed, the CRC churches in Englewood instituted a policy of interviewing African American (but not white) visitors after church services "to consider with them their motivation."[130] First Englewood CRC locked its doors immediately after the beginning of service to keep African Americans from joining worship.[131] All three of the Englewood CRC churches left the neighborhood between 1962 and 1964.

For a little while, the four CRC churches in Roseland supported the Pullman Gospel Center, a nearby organization that had recently begun serving the African American population. The churches seemed to want an outpost, or "mission," in the community they were leaving behind.[132] But this did not last long. In 1971, when only Fourth Roseland had announced plans to move, the Roseland CRC churches recommended that the mission come under the responsibility of the

---

[126] Mark T. Mulder, *Shades of White Flight: Evangelical Congregations and Urban Departure* (New Brunswick, NJ: Rutgers University Press, 2015), 32–33.
[127] Mulder, *Shades of White Flight*, 34.
[128] Mulder, *Shades of White Flight*, 34–41.
[129] Mulder, *Shades of White Flight*, 69.
[130] Mulder, *Shades of White Flight*, 80.
[131] Mulder, *Shades of White Flight*, 80.
[132] Mulder, *Shades of White Flight*, 87, 94–95.

CRC Home Mission Board, wiping their hands of the center.[133] By the following year, all four of the Roseland CRC churches were gone.

My purpose in recounting this story is not to single out the CRC. I have focused on this community because its actions were representative and not unusual among white Christian responses to demographic changes. It is one thing for a church to affirm the fellowship that all Christians share in the Spirit. It is another to ask how particular communities have responded to minorities in their midst. The effects of such decisions remain in the condescension, marginalization, and sometimes explicit racism that minorities frequently experience in white Chicagoland churches. There is a social history to the forms of segregation that continue to define Christianity today.

Conclusion

In *The Christian Imagination*, Willie Jennings writes:

> Where we live determines in great measure how we live. Where we agree to the spatial configurations of the land inevitably means a tacit agreement to the racial formation of the world. We must enter the struggle of land acquisition, space and place design, targeted housing development, buying, and selling which constantly reestablishes and strengthens segregationist mentalities and racial identities...[134]

The CRC's flight from Chicago illustrates Jennings's point. The problem with ecclesial segregation is not homogeneity itself. It is the social and historical realities that these homogeneities represent. The Christian color line is not an accident of history or the innocent effect of individuals worshipping where they feel most

---
[133] Mulder, *Shades of White Flight*, 92.
[134] Willie James Jennings, *The Christian Imagination: Theology and the Origins of Race* (New Haven, CT: Yale University Press, 2011), 287.

comfortable. It is the legacy of white Christian populations repudiating their minority, and especially Black, brothers and sisters. Social and historical analysis exposes the degree to which our communities have been shaped by demographic change, racial prejudice, and concerns about property values and school district lines. Separations of geography, race, and class reflect and exacerbate the antagonism of Christians against one another. No serious effort to bridge our color lines can ignore the social and material conditions that fuel racial division. The doctrinal identity of racially divided Christians requires critical examination of the places that separate us and the modes of oppression they represent.

These Black Dry Bones Will Live Again: A Pneumatological Ideation of the Black Church's Liberation from Social Death

Leon Harris

The church in the U.S. is floundering. This is a well-known fact among Christian academics and is attested in Pew Research, PRRI, and Barna Research.[135] The number of those who consider themselves religiously unaffiliated continues to grow. Unfortunately, the cause of the current anti-church sentiment has also impacted the state of the Black Church, especially among our young folk. Carter Woodson says: "It is very clear, then, that if Negroes got their conception of religion from slaveholders, libertines, and murderers, there may be something wrong about it, and it would not hurt to investigate it."[136] For Woodson, the theological education Black Americans received from white schools of theology did not prepare them to serve and

---

[135] "About Three-in-Ten U.S. Adults Are Now Religiously Unaffiliated," Dec. 14, 2021. Pew Research Center. https://www.pewresearch.org/religion/2021/12/14/about-three-in-ten-u-s-adults-are-now-religiously-unaffiliated/ (accessed March 1, 2023).; "Religion and Congregations in a Time of Social and Political Upheaval," May 16, 2023. Public Religion Research Institute. https://www.prri.org/research/religion-and-congregations-in-a-time-of-social-and-political-upheaval/.

[136] Carter G. Woodson, *Mis-Education of the Negro* (Drewryville, VA: Khalifah's Booksellers & Associates, 2005), 73.

uplift their Black congregations properly. Woodson averred that due to Black ministers whom white theology schools trained, many Black youth no longer look to the Church as a place of relevance, so they leave it. Unfortunately, the situation today is not much different, and it feels safe to say that things are monumentally worse. Part of the problem is that a theological education devoid of a Gospel of liberation that originates from within the Black Christian experience creates a sense of enslavement instead of the liberation that Christ gives us.

The concept of theological social death explains this sense of enslavement. It is social death because the personhood of the Black Christian qua Black Christian does not exist in the hallowed halls of predominantly white schools of theology. The work of Orlando Patterson provides the definition and patterns for explicating the idea of social death. Using Patterson's work, this paper will connect *Slavery as Social Death* to a theological social death. Due to space, this work will be limited to an exploration of four primary themes: 1) Slavery as the maintenance of natal alienation and dishonor; 2) Slavery as a relationship of dominance that leads to social death; 3) Two conceptions of social death, and 4) Honor and degradation in the master-slave relation. These four themes will serve as a framework to understand how social death is limited to those physically enslaved. However, social death is also a theological possibility when pneumatological liberty is withheld from God's people.

Slavery as the Maintenance of Natal Alienation and Dishonor

Slavery is typically understood as total dominance and control over another human being, usually for economic or labor purposes. For Patterson, the problem with this definition is that a new personhood category is unnecessary. In other words, someone in prison is under the complete control of another individual, yet the prisoner is not a slave because even prisoners have rights. In some societies, a wife has little to no control over her life, but she would not consider herself a slave. For Patterson, "slavery is the permanent, violent domination of natally alienated and generally dishonored persons."[137] The concept of "natal alienation" is the drive to ensure the slave's continual existence as one without a natal origin and in a perpetual state of dishonor that creates slavery. The slave is denied and alienated from all rights or claims of birth experienced by all members of society due to a given and assumed genealogical heritage of being human. In other words, society recognizes that everyone has some lineage as part of an individual's genealogically historic connections within the human social order—basically, you know where you come from. Slaves were not allowed to know their past as a connection with their current reality or integrate their experiences into society freely. Moreover, they were not allowed to integrate the knowledge of their ancestors into their lives—the slave's past does not inform their current reality. Without history, slaves existed only *in* and *from* their master's history or genealogy. The result is a denial of the slave's human birthright, typically presumed by other humans, thereby making the slave nonhuman. The slaves become perpetual outsiders who have lost birth ties from ascending and descending generations—no past or future heritage. The drive for the relationship of dominance derives from the master's need for honor and recognition, which comes about by dishonoring the slave's existence and even the slave's fight for her human dignity and honor. Eventually, the mechanisms to maintain the slave's condition of natal alienation and dishonor are embedded within the very social structures created by the masters. Once the master-slave relationship becomes institutionalized, the structures are in place to ensure the slave's status as natally alienated, and the strictures also

---

[137] Orlando Patterson, *Slavery and Social Death: A Comparative Study*, First edition (Cambridge, MA: Harvard University Press, 2018), 13.

ensure the loss of honor. The goal of the institutionalized structures and strictures is a dialectical paradox that establishes the slave's natal alienation and loss of honor. It is a paradox because the individual's natal alienation and loss of honor create a slave, but then, the system is simultaneously embedded with the mechanisms to create and maintain natal alienation and loss of honor. This paradoxical dialectic works to secure the master's ultimate goal for the slave: social death.

Slavery as a Relationship of Dominance That Leads to Social Death

It is not just dominance over another that constitutes slavery; the slave is socially powerless in relation to the person considered their master. The slave's personhood is no longer constituted within the structures of being a human entity—that is, those constitutive elements endowed by the Creator. This way, the slave does not exist apart from their master; the slave's existence is only through the lens of the master. Christian Smith says that "persons... are originally, constitutively, and inescapably social, interactive, and communicative in origin and being. Sociality helps constitute the essential character of personhood."[138] The aspect of being a thoroughly socialized being to ensure personhood is denied to the enslaved person, especially in relation to their master and society at large. Patterson says, "because the slave had no socially recognized existence outside of his master, he became a social nonperson."[139] The slave had no self-agency at any social level outside of their master. This way, the slave lacks the socially constituted elements for full personhood to the point that the slave is a nonperson. At this point, the slave is now conceived, treated,

---

[138] Christian Smith, *What Is a Person?: Rethinking Humanity, Social Life, and the Moral Good from the Person Up* (Chicago, IL: University of Chicago Press, 2010), 67.
[139] Patterson, *Slavery and Social Death*, 5.

constituted, and obtains a self-image as socially dead: social death is essential for being a slave.

Social death is insufficient to cement a person's status as a slave; natal alienation is an insidious repudiation of a person's historical moorings. All members of society are assumed to have a genealogical heritage that determines their existence as human beings. However, the slave is denied and alienated from all rights or claims of birth experienced by those granted genealogical heritage. In other words, everyone has some lineage that is respected as part of the historical movement of the human social order. Slaves were not allowed to know their past as a connection with their current reality. By not allowing a free integration of their experiences and knowledge of their ancestors into their lives, the slaves' history does not inform their reality. Without history, slaves existed only in and from their master's history or genealogy, which eventually denies the slaves' normal human birthrights, thereby making the slave a nonhuman. The slaves become perpetual outsiders who have lost birth ties from ascending and descending generations. According to Patterson, "The incapacity to make any claims of birth or to pass on such claims is considered a natural injustice among all peoples, so that those who were obliged to suffer it had to be regarded as somehow socially dead."[140] The odious nature of natal alienation is the denial of the slave's humanity, the denial of any independent social existence apart from the master. For all injustices against the slave are no longer defined as injustices against a person. Natal alienation means the slave is socially and culturally dead. Therefore, since injustices cannot occur against a nonperson, the slave then has no inalienable claim for justice based on being part of the human race.

For Patterson, the third constituent element of the slave relation stems from "the fact that slaves were always persons who had been dishonored in a generalized way."[141] Since the slave has no natal origin

---

[140] Patterson, *Slavery and Social Death*, 8.
[141] Patterson, *Slavery and Social Death*, 11.

and their personhood is solely dependent on the master, the slave lives in a perpetual state of nonhonor. The slave is permanently indebted to their master, a life without inherent worth or honor is a life of indignity. Due to the slave's lack of independent social existence, the slave has no public worth and, therefore, no public honor. Since the slave has no honor to defend, they could only defend their master's name. The slave's ontology is embedded in a display of "outward self-hatred in the presence of the master, which was prompted by the pervasive indignity and underlying physical violence of the relationship."[142] Survival in the face of indignity and violence means that the slave must learn to venerate the honor of the master while denigrating the humanity of all slaves as nonpersons without power, natal origin, or honor.

The Loss of Communal Participation as Social Death

The loss of power, natal origin, and honor leads to social death due to the total loss of existing as an equal member of a socially recognized community—that is, a member of a community with its sense of self-determination, self-definition, and history. A person is an individual who participates within a complex network of socially recognized individuals, either as equals or hierarchically. This gives purpose, identity, status, and historical origin that cements a continuity of identity to an individual. So, after the slave loses power, natal origin, and honor, the depersonalized and desocialized slave is then introduced into the community of their master but not as a social person, as a nonsocial being. This is nonbeing or social death: "Identity is a phenomenon that emerges from the dialectic between individual and society. On the other hand, identity types are social products *tout court*, relatively stable elements of objective reality (the degree of stability being, of course, socially

---

[142] Patterson, *Slavery and Social Death*, 12.

determined in its turn)."[143] These "*types*" loosely correspond to the person within a given social network, so that one *type* is to be a socially alive person and another is to be socially dead or a nonbeing. For Patterson, the social type is constructed in societies by using customs, laws, and ideology forced upon the enslaved individual and agreed upon by the dominant group members. These socially constructed ideologies establish the permanent position of the slave as a nonparticipant in the construction of the self, which is the definition of being socially dead.

Honor and Degradation in the Master-Slave Relation

One essential element that constitutes a person as a slave is not ultimate power over an individual but the conferring of dishonor. Patterson argues that in all slave societies, a slave was considered a degraded person, not simply someone who had lost ultimate power. By degrading the person, the master's honor is enhanced by the subjection of his slave. In order to maintain the dishonor of the slave and the honor of the master, the dominant slaveholding society would conceive of itself as a decent society, which further cemented the reality of honor and dishonor in the master-slave relation. Since honor is something every human desires, once a person is denied the ability to compete for honor, that person is socially dead. In other words, for a person to obtain honor, they must have the power to have their honor accepted or at least the power to claim that their acts should be considered honorable. It is also essential for the master to embark on a campaign of demeaning the slave using various labels and stereotypes to ensure the subjugation of the slave. The slave's honor is only maintained through the connection with the master. The master needs the slave to maintain their status as a person of honor. The use of the slave as the permanent definition of dishonor is the ultimate experience of social death as a nonbeing.

---

[143] Peter L. Berger and Thomas Luckmann, *The Social Construction of Reality: A Treatise in the Sociology of Knowledge* (Albany, NY: Anchor Books, 1990), 174.

Natal Alienation and Dishonor as the Constitutive Elements of Theological Social Death

At this point, Patterson is moving beyond the limiting definition of slavery as mere control over another for economic gains. Patterson ultimately refers to slavery as parasitism. Patterson explains: "On this intersubjective level the slaveholder fed on the slave to gain the very direct satisfactions of power over another, honor enhancement, and authority. The slave, losing in the process all claim to autonomous power, was degraded and reduced to a state of liminality."[144]

During the development of the Western theological imagination, Black Theology lost autonomy. The dominant culture deemed Black Theology as illegitimate. Black Theology exists in a contentious liminal space, striving for survival. The white, Western theological project is "In practice—a god. Not *the* God. But the very modern form of god-in-the-flesh. The very epitome (scandalously!) of Christianity—incarnation caricatured—the Jesus-God of the blue eye and fair hair. Whiteness is first of all 'theological.'" [145] The Black Church and, by extension, Black Theology have been relegated to a condition of perpetual subjugation to the white theological imagination because the Black Church is judged by its adherence to white European theologies. This subjugation ultimately leads to a theological social death for the existence and identity of the Black Church *qua* Black Church in Jesus Christ.

Theological Slavery as a Relationship of Dominance That Leads to Theological Social Death

Recalling that the first constituent element of the slave relation is powerlessness in relation to another individual, it is not a stretch of

---

[144] Patterson, *Slavery and Social Death*, 337.
[145] James W. Perkinson, *White Theology: Outing Supremacy in Modernity*, First edition (New York, NY: Palgrave Macmillan, 2004), 192.

the imagination to realize that Black theological thought is powerless in predominantly white Christian institutions in the U.S. According to the Association of Theological Schools, approximately 7% of faculty in member schools are Black Non-Hispanic.[146] For example, at the time of this writing, reviewing the websites of nine of the top seminaries (see below)[147] in the U.S., there are only five Black American deans and no Black Americans serving as chairs combined at these schools. Two exceptions: at the time of this writing, both Fuller Seminary and Princeton Theological Seminary had just hired Black American presidents. Things are not much better at Christian colleges: "The data show that the percentage of African Americans employed at CCCU institutions in full-time management, which includes cabinet members, as well as, directors, deans, and associate vice presidents was 4.19% in 2016."[148] The point is that without the power to influence white institutions, the Black Church and Theology will continue to be in a permanent state of powerlessness in relation to the dominant theological ideology of a white ethnocentric worldview.

Theological Slavery as Theological Natal Alienation

A rich theological Christian heritage began on the African continent and reinvented itself from within the atrocities of the Occidental enslavement of Black people. Having had the opportunity to serve in Biola's Division of Diversity and Inclusion, I reviewed the curriculum of Biola

---

[146] "Personnel (Faculty and Administrators)," ATS Resources, https://www.ats.edu/Data-Visualization.

[147] The schools I reviewed are Dallas Theological Seminary, Duke Divinity School, Fuller Theological Seminary, Gordon-Conwell Theological Seminary, North Park Theological Seminary, Princeton Theological Seminary, Talbot School of Theology, Southern Baptist Theological Seminary (Louisville, KY), and Trinity Evangelical Divinity School. To be fair, it is possible that all chairs are not listed on the schools' websites.

[148] Marlowe V.N. Washington, "Experiences of African American Mid-Level Leaders in the Council for Christian College and Universities: A Phenomenological Approach to Diversity" Ed.D. dissertation (St. John Fisher University, 2019), 15, https://fisherpub.sjf.edu/education_etd/427.

and other Council for Christian Colleges and Universities (CCCUs). It is apparent that Black Church history in the U.S. is not required. In most CCCUs, it is not even an elective. Allan Boesak states:

> What must be considered one of the most significant events in the history of the Christian church, the Reformation, bypassed completely the black situation, and neither the Roman Catholic church nor the new Protestant churches endeavored to make black reality part of the fundamental changes which had occurred then. Indeed, the Reformation did not change anything about the lot whites had prepared for black people.[149]

Denying the Black Church's theological heritage and theology constitutes a theological natal alienation. Black folks' theological heritage is not derived from within but from a white framework. It is no longer Jesus Christ who informs the Black Church but a racialized system of stratification that engages in cultural rituals such as microaggressions, racelighting, and hegemonic control over intellectual thought to ensure that Blackness has no claims to Christian history in the West. Willie Jennings says:

> Crudely put, theological education vacillates between a pedagogical imagination calibrated to forming white self-sufficient men and a related pedagogical imagination calibrated to forming a Christian racial and cultural homogeneity that yet performs the nationalist vision of that same white self-sufficient man. Theological education, however, is simply living out in microcosm the wider problem that plagues Western education.[150]

---

[149] Allan Boesak, *Farewell to Innocence: A Socio-Ethical Study on Black Theology and Black Power* (Eugene, OR: Wipf & Stock, 2015), 31.
[150] Willie James Jennings, *After Whiteness: An Education in Belonging* (Grand Rapids, MI: William B. Eerdmans Publishing Company, 2020).

Christian history and theology are taught from a particular social location that began in Rome and ends in contemporary Western society. The Black Church is simply a footnote at best and an outlier at worst that must be critiqued and corrected. The paternalistic attitude toward the theological heritage of the Black Church and Theology creates theological natal alienation due to the assumption that Black Christians owe their theological heritage to the Gospel of the Occident. This paternalistic attitude toward Black Theology completes the second constituent element for theological slavery: instead of Christ alone, it is the Occident and Christ alone.

Theological Slavery as Theological Dishonor

One of the critical elements of slavery is to deny the possibility of honor within a person or group, but this is not enough to complete the social death of the person or group. The other critical element needed to complete the social death of the enslaved is to ensure that the enslaved person's (or group's) honor is located in another person or group that is deemed worthy of honor, usually the master. The posture within primarily white Christian schools of theology is that color blindness is the proper method to do theology. These institutions assert that they are participating in a universal theology beyond any cultural context. By many estimations, this is nothing more than a self-justifying claim that ignores the simple reality that no one can escape their cultural influences and location. The underlying theological framework of these institutions is the celebration of the achievement of white theologians through the framework of meritocracy and America's doctrine of Manifest Destiny. It is the duty of the Black academic studying in these institutions to learn, appreciate, and ultimately celebrate the theological greatness of Luther, Calvin, Edwards, Francis Schaeffer, John Piper, Tillich, Barth, R.C. Sproul, B.B. Warfield, Billy Graham, and the like. Not only that, but it is also the Black student's job to learn to use these great people as the sole criterion to offer critiques of the Black Church. Critical engagement is nothing more than a cipher that means judging the Black Church based on the writing and thoughts of all these white men who have nothing positive to say or even nothing at all to say about the Black Church apart from white Christianity[151].

Theological Slavery as the Loss of Participation Toward Theological Social Death

Ecclesiology is the idea that the Church is the People of God formed as the Body of Christ to be the People of the Holy Spirit. It is the Apostle Paul who said,

> But God has so arranged the body, giving the greater honour to the inferior member, that there may be no dissension within the body, but the members may have the same care for one another. If one member suffers, all suffer together with it; if one member is honored, all rejoice together with it.[152]

H. Richard Niebuhr says that,

> Denominationalism in the Christian church is such an unacknowledged hypocrisy… It represents the accommodation of Christianity to the caste-system of human society. It carries over into the organization of the Christian principle of brotherhood the prides and prejudices, the privilege and prestige, as well as the humiliations and abasements, the injustices and

---

[151] According to an article by Michael Emerson: "Through extensive statistical analyses, we found that two-thirds of practicing white Christians are following, in effect, a religion of whiteness. They repeatedly placed being white ahead of being Christian; the findings were not explained away by political affiliation, location, age, education, income, gender, or other factors." See Michael O. Emerson, "What Happens When White Identity Comes Before Christian Faith?" July 2022. *Sojourners Magazine*. https://sojo.net/magazine/july-2022/what-happens-when-white-identity-comes-christian-faith (accessed March 30, 2023).
[152] 1 Cor. 12:24–26.

inequalities of the specious order of high and low wherein men find the satisfaction of their craving for vainglory. The division of the churches closely follows the division of men into the castes of national, racial, and economic groups. It draws the color line in the church of God...[153]

Niebuhr wrote this in 1922, and not much has changed since. For example, Robert P. Jones says that "most white Christian churches continue to serve, consciously or not, as the mechanisms for transmitting and reinforcing white supremacist attitudes among new generations."[154] This means that part of the Black Church is experiencing a theological social death due to its socialized conditioning that its theological developments must occur within, or at the least by the approval of, predominantly white Christian institutions. The particularity of the Black Church—a tradition that emerged in response to the dehumanizing ideology of white supremacy—is either absorbed or discarded by so-called neutral theological projects, which is a forced universalism grounded in the particular traditions of Anglo-European churches. The traditions of the Protestant churches in the West did not consider the ideas of non-European individuals as valid or essential: Black Christians were theologically and societally dead during the formation of the Protestant traditions. This intentional exclusion of non-European voices is one of many reasons white Christians justified the enslavement of Africans. They could not perceive these theological outsiders as true Christians because they did not follow the practices and did not submit to the authority of their churches. Consequently, these nonparticipants in the culture of white Christianity were not persons; they were nonbeings. For the particularity given to the Black theologians by Christ to be recovered, Black theologians

---

[153] H. Richard Niebuhr, *The Social Sources of Denominationalism* (New York, NY: Meridian Books, 1962), 6.
[154] Robert P. Jones, *White Too Long: The Legacy of White Supremacy in American Christianity* (New York, NY: Simon & Schuster, 2020), 186.

in *all* Christian institutions must be allowed to participate as equals. The particularity of Black theologians (and the Black Church) is an outcome of the particularizing work of the Holy Spirit, who is moving creation to the eschatological diversity that is the Kingdom of the triune God.

Recommendations for Liberation from Theological Social Death

"Where the Spirit of the Lord is, there is freedom."[155] Dwight Hopkins views the work of the triune God as liberation for the oppressed. Hopkins says, "God, in constructive black theology, is the Spirit of total liberation for us. Jesus is the fulfillment of the Spirit of total liberation revealed to be with us. And human purpose is the Spirit of total liberation in us."[156] In order to be liberated from theological social death, we must fully embrace a Gospel Haymanot that derives its trajectory from within the complete revelation of the God of deliverance whom Israel experienced; the God who is fully revealed as the holistic deliverer in Jesus Christ. If Gospel Haymanot is "a principal characteristic of African-American Christians since our ethnogenesis,"[157] then we must retrieve and fully embrace the "unique liturgical traditions that have developed in the context of oppression."[158] To this end, I have a few personal reflections and recommendations as a member of the theological academy.

In order to liberate ourselves from theological social death, there must be a recognition that, as Black Gospelist theologians, we have been formed by the demands of a system that was never designed for our benefit. In many cases, our capitulation to this system was a matter

---

[155] 2 Cor. 3:17
[156] Dwight N. Hopkins, *Down, Up, and Over: Slave Religion and Black Theology* (Minneapolis, MN: Fortress Press, 1999), 158.
[157] Vince L. Bantu, *Gospel Haymanot: A Constructive Theology and Critical Reflection on African and Diasporic Christianity* (Calumet City, IL: Urban Ministries, Inc., 2020), 9.
[158] Bantu, *Gospel Haymanot*, 9.

of survival; but it is time to recognize the system for what it is: the near-total disregard for the plight of Black folk. In order to liberate ourselves, we must develop alternative means of instruction for Black students and means of remuneration for Black academics. Let us return to the strategy of our ancestors during their enslavement and invest in generational liberation. In other words, let us begin developing theological schools, publishing houses, and unabashedly Black conferences.

We must also develop a Gospel Haymanot curriculum that details the rich theological heritage of the Black Church and those ancestors from the African continent. We must demonstrate that the risen Christ alone has called us into His kingdom; we stand by the Reformation's declaration of *Solus Christus* ("by Christ alone"). We must also stress the continual remembrance of the oppressive history of the Western Christian church toward Blacks all over the globe. Remembering is not enough; we must critically examine the theological developments of those so-called Christian fathers—like the slaveowner Jonathan Edwards, whose theology did not give the resources to fight for Black liberation and equality. It is time that, instead of appealing to European Church fathers as if they are some divinely ordained eternal authorities, we return to the authority of Jesus Christ's calling that gives us the privilege and right to speak about what part of the tradition is valid or invalid.

Finally, we should not allow the dominant theological narrative to frighten us from standing in solidarity with other Black theologians because they make white males uncomfortable. If we judge our Black theologians based on the theological methods and posture of white theologians alone, it is as if we are using the master's tools to gain our freedom. Our honor is a divinely granted privilege in Jesus Christ by the Holy Spirit; it is not given through the so-called hallowed halls of white academia. We no longer judge theologians like James Cone through the authority of John MacArthur and others who consider him heretical. We judge James Cone based on the standards of a Gospel Haymanot, a Gospel that originates from within the location of Black oppression.

For example, Cone says, "although most biblical scholars rightly question the historical validity of the birth narratives in Matthew and Luke, the mythic value of these stories is important theologically."[159] Gospel Haymanot takes seriously the revelation of scripture, so it must reject Cone's view that the birth narratives are primarily theological or symbolic, meaning the historicity of the narratives is either secondary or to be rejected. The birth narratives for Gospel Haymanot are divine actions of the Holy Spirit in Jesus Christ, which took place in history, to inaugurate the re-creation event in the redemptive work of Jesus Christ. The birth narratives are both historically and theologically important and revelatory. On the other hand, Cone states:

> Continuing the Exodus-Sinai and David-Zion traditions in which there is special connection between divine revelation and the poor, the early Church remembered Jesus' historical person as exemplifying the same character. That character, they concluded, *must* have been present in his birth. This is the significance of the birth stories in Matthew and Luke, the Son of God Christology in Mark, and the Fourth Gospel's contention that "When all things began, the Word already was" (1:1 NEB). The four Gospels intend to express divine purpose; and the content of the purpose is disclosed clearly in the Magnificat…[160]

Since Gospel Haymanot is concerned with Blacks' liberation from oppression, it agrees with Cone's point regarding Mary's Magnificat. Mary's Magnificat is an expression of God's activity in Jesus Christ through the Holy Spirit inaugurating an era of divine liberation for the oppressed and powerless. A deliverance that takes place in *this* world

---

[159] James H. Cone, *A Black Theology of Liberation*, Fortieth anniversary edition (Maryknoll, NY: Orbis Books, 2010), 120.
[160] James H. Cone, *God of the Oppressed*, Revised edition (Maryknoll, NY: Orbis Books, 1997), 67.

both vertically and horizontally: vertically speaking, deliverance from an alienated state with God; horizontally speaking, deliverance from oppressive social structures, especially racism as experienced in the U.S. This does not mean God is only reaching out to the materially poor and socially weak but that there is a recognition that God's justice in Jesus Christ includes the restoration of equality and equity in God's community, which should be expressed in the church of Jesus Christ. The point here is that Black theologians are not immature children waiting for our parents to approve our theology. Black theologians have the same right and privilege to develop, judge, investigate, accept, or reject theologians just like any white theologian.

In conclusion, the goal of overcoming a theological, social death is for all the Black Church to live the abundant life that Jesus promised in John 10:10. By overcoming social death, the Black Church and community in all its varied forms and identities can be part of the eschatological vision of the heavenly city where "the glory and honor of the nations will be brought into it." (Rev. 21:26) The benefit of escaping a theological social death is that everyone can participate in a Gospel Haymanot. All communities can become the eschatological Kingdom that the Holy Spirit creates within each community as a universal expression of the Body of Christ. By recognizing the Holy Spirit's work in the Black Church and other communities, even those who were either perpetrators or complicit in maintaining white theological hegemony can repent and join us in working toward the liberation of all. There are no outsiders in God's desire to deliver His people; everyone can be liberators as copartners with the liberating Spirit of Jesus Christ.

Black Marriage as Social Justice

Preston and Charonda Boone

"Let us rejoice and be glad
and give him the glory,
because the wedding celebration of the Lamb has come,
and his bride has prepared herself.
And it has been granted to her that she be dressed in bright,
clean fine linen (for the fine linen is the righteous deeds
of the saints)."[161]

"To be clear, the answer to systemic racism is not Black marriage. But strong Black families are a form of resistance… When your cultural history includes familial ties ripped apart, force-bred for profit, and dehumanized, marriage remains powerful and important."
Dr. Christina Edmondson[162]

Introduction

The triune God of the Bible is a God of covenant righteousness. One way that God expresses this righteousness in and among His human

---

[161] Rev. 19:7–8
[162] Christina Edmonson, "I's Married Now: Christian Marriage for Grown Black Women," *Truth's Table: Black Women's Musings on Life, Love, and Liberation*, eds. Ekemini Uwan et al. (New York: Convergent, 2022), 148.

image-bearers[163] is through marriage. This paper will explore the theological, historical, and social viability of marriage as an instrument and expression of God's justice in human families, communities, and cultures. The focus will be on African-diasporic populations in the United States. We argue that Black marriage and social justice can intersect in ways that holistically empower individuals, couples, and communities. Using a gospelist framework,[164] marriage-as-social-justice combines Scripture's recognition of marriage as honorable[165] with a concern for the flourishing of African Americans as resisters of oppression. We will offer biblical, theological, and sociological arguments to support this thesis before lifting up just a few historical case studies of Black marriages that contributed to Black flourishing.

Marriage

Marriage is defined as a socially recognized union of one man and one woman forming a basic unit of a familial structure.[166] The Bible presents marriage as "an estate of life founded in the creation itself that persists in all cultures despite corruptions introduced by sinful humanity."[167] This paper will assume a biblical sexual ethic, which restricts marriage to a covenant between one man and one woman.

---

[163] "Human image-bearers" may seem redundant, but Preston sees divine beings as bearing the imago dei, as well (Gen. 1:26; cf. Michael S. Heiser, *The Unseen Realm: Recovering the Supernatural Worldview of the Bible*, First edition (Bellingham, WA: Lexham Press, 2015), 38. Marriage, however, is only for humans (cf. Lk 2:34–36). The "marriages" of divine beings with humans in Gen. 6:1–6 were illegitimate and therefore grieved God.

[164] All of this is consistent with Gospel Haymanot, which "holds firmly to the authority of the divinely inspired Word of God and its call for justice for all of God's creation." Vince L. Bantu, "An Introduction to Gospel Haymanot," *Gospel Haymanot: A Constructive Theology and Critical Reflection on African and Diasporic Christianity,* ed. Vince L. Bantu (Chicago: Urban Ministries, Inc., 2020), 10.

[165] Heb. 13:4

[166] Jonathan D. Redding, "Marriage," *Lexham Theological Wordbook*, eds. Douglas Mangum et al., (Bellingham, WA: Lexham Press, 2014).

[167] Jonathan Warren P. (Pagán), "Marriage," *Lexham Survey of Theology*, eds. Mark Ward et al. (Bellingham, WA: Lexham Press, 2018).

Marriage and justice are interwoven with creation and new creation. Marriage is instituted at creation and points to the eschatological union of Christ and the church—new creation. Injustice creates enmity between humans and creation[168] and requires eschatological resolution—the righteous kingdom of God in the new creation, the marriage of heaven and earth. In the meantime, marital covenants operate as a space of sanctification and edification for human persons. Marriage sanctifies and edifies.

Social Justice

Theologian B. P. Irwin writes that, in the Hebrew Bible, social justice is primarily associated with resisting inequity against society's most vulnerable members, both relationally and with an eye toward cosmic consequences.[169]

Adapting Irwin for the contemporary context, we define social justice in this article as justice for the most vulnerable members of North American society. The Bible depicts social justice and marriage as related in imagery and missional vision. For Israel, social justice was a function of covenant obligation.[170] Several times in the prophetic books of the Hebrew Scriptures, God's covenant with Israel is likened to a marriage (e.g., Jer. 3; 31:31–33; Is. 54:5; 62:5; Ezek. 16; Hos. 2). A covenant is a sacred bond of kinship between two parties sealed by law and liturgy.[171] Israel's sin is often cast as adultery (Jer 3; Hos 2). Specifically, the social injustices of Israel's rulers are compared to marital infidelities. This is clear in the book of Hosea, where God and His prophet not only use the language of adultery to condemn

---

[168] Gen. 3:17–19; Lev. 18:28
[169] B. P. Irwin, "Social Justice." *Dictionary of the Old Testament: Prophets*, eds. Mark J. Boda and J. Gordon McConville (Downers Grove, IL: IVP Academic, 2012), 719.
[170] Irwin, "Social Justice," 721.
[171] Scott Hahn, "Covenant," *The Lexham Bible Dictionary*, eds. John D. Barry et al. (Bellingham, WA: Lexham Press, 2016).

Judah's idolatry but also that nation's *injustice*.¹⁷² Justice, broadly, is that which promotes equity among humans.¹⁷³ It often entails a reversal of fortunes, a divine "[uplifting of] the righteous and oppressed and debasing [of] the unrighteous and oppressors."¹⁷⁴ This uplifting encompasses both localized actions—such as Boaz redeeming Ruth and Naomi from poverty by marrying Ruth¹⁷⁵—and larger-scale policies—such as the Mosaic Law Year of Jubilee with its leveling of the economic playing field.¹⁷⁶

The Practical Intersection: Black Marriage and Black Flourishing

The intersection of Black Marriage and social justice is Black flourishing. Healthy Black marriages do justice to Black people insofar as they contribute to the spiritual, psychological, sociological, and economic wellness of Black people and their communities.

The Apostle Paul reveals the submission and reverence that a man and woman should show each other, not only as a married couple but also as siblings in Christ (Eph. 5:21). On the household scale, marriage can position husbands and wives to practice justice: It calls husbands and wives to render godly action toward—or judgment of—one another. The mutual vulnerability of marriage lays bare the sin of each spouse, creating opportunities for each spouse to forgive and confront the other. This judgment is only godly insofar as it is loving and gracious, calling the spouse (further) into godliness and away from sin.

Marriage-as-justice affirms and honors the spouse's virtue, and it rejects the spouse's sin—all while maintaining loyal love and kindness (hesed) to the spouse. In his book *How to Fight Racism*, Jemar

---

¹⁷² Hos. 1–2; Irwin, "Social Justice"
¹⁷³ Jeremiah K. Garrett, "Justice."*The Lexham Bible Dictionary,* eds. John D. Barry et al. (Bellingham, WA: Lexham Press, 2016).
¹⁷⁴ Garrett, "Justice"
¹⁷⁵ Ru. 4:9–10
¹⁷⁶ Lev. 25:8–55

Tisby draws upon psychologist John Gottman's marriage research and applies it to racial justice: Gottman claims that contempt, stemming from "a sense of superiority" and "disrespect," is toxic to marriages. Tisby then points out that "The damaging effects of contempt apply not only to marriage but to racial justice as well. We must constantly check our hearts to ensure that we are not demonstrating contempt for others. The temptation to look down on others because of their backward views on race and diversity easily descends into disdain and haughtiness."[177] We posit that marriage helps to mold (Black Christian) people to engage in the work of social justice in a way that glorifies God. Marriage can be a crucible for building the godly character and virtue that strengthens a gospelist witness in the public square. Marriage and advocacy are both tools for and fruits of sanctification.

Psychological & Sociological Flourishing

Black marriage provides emotional support. Married couples report higher levels of trust and satisfaction as opposed to couples who cohabit.[178] Parental marriage appears to be especially important for the well-being of young African American males. In areas of parental support, delinquency, self-esteem, and school performance, having one's father in the home, and particularly one's married father, appears to be a crucial determinant of better outcomes for young Black males.[179] In general, Black men benefit more from marriage than do Black women in terms of health.[180] This finding suggests that marriage

---

[177] Jemar Tisby, *How to Fight Racism: Courageous Christianity and the Journey Toward Racial Justice* (Grand Rapids, MI: Zondervan Reflective, 2021), 281–282.
[178] Juliana Menasce Horowitz, Nikki Graf, and Gretchen Livingston, "Marriage and Cohabitation in the U.S." November 6, 2019. Pew Research Center. https://www.pewresearch.org/social-trends/2019/11/06/marriage-and-cohabitation-in-the-u-s/. (accessed August 2022).
[179] Lorraine Blackman, Obie Clayton, Norval Glenn, Linda Malone-Colon, and Alex Roberts, *The Consequences of Marriage for African Americans: A Comprehensive Literature Review* (New York: Institute for American Values, 2005), 6.
[180] Blackman et al., *The Consequences of Marriage for African Americans*, 5.

is particularly important for African American males at all stages of the life cycle.[181] Marriage does justice to children—often the most vulnerable humans—by providing them with stability and structure. Unfortunately, this is often seen more clearly in the absence of marriage and its benefits. Vince Bacote draws attention to this in his book, *The Political Disciple: A Theology of Public Life*:

> The instability of the relationships among the parents plays a significant role in reducing the chances of later success in life for these children, which ultimately contributes to an ongoing crisis for society, one that calls for various public strategies.[182]

Thus, Black parenting by way of healthy Black marriages has an impact on economic flourishing and community viability. Marriage does justice to communities. It has the potential to create social cohesion in families and local communities (i.e., neighborhoods, towns, and villages). Bacote argues that the wealth gap between rich and poor is exacerbated by marriage rates declining most sharply among the poor.[183] If this is true, then it follows that Black marriage can help in the fight against the growing racial wage gap.

Cohabitation is on the rise, and finances is one of the major reasons why partners state they will not say "I do," as they saw a lack of financial readiness in themselves or in their partners.[184] Yet, married Black adults, compared to those who are unmarried, have more income, are less likely to face poverty, and are more likely to express life satisfaction.[185]

---

[181] Ibid., 5.
[182] Vincent Bacote, *The Political Disciple: A Theology of Public Life* (Grand Rapids, MI: Zondervan, 2015), 86.
[183] Bacote, *Political Disciple*, 87
[184] Nikki Graf, "Key findings on marriage and cohabitation in the U.S.," November 6, 2019. Pew Research Center. https://www.pewresearch.org/fact-tank/2019/11/06/key-findings-on-marriage-and-cohabitation-in-the-u-s/. (accessed August 19, 2022).
[185] Blackman et al., *The Consequences of Marriage for African Americans*, 6.

Black Marriage in Historical Context

Marriage is one of the main institutions that the U.S. government values. Yet today, African Americans are significantly less likely than any other racial/ethnic group to ever marry; less likely to remarry; more likely to divorce, separate, and cohabit; and more likely to bear and rear children out of wedlock.[186] Overall, in the past 50+ years, U.S. marriage has steeply declined. Across all ethnic groups, in 1970, 28.1% of men were never married, and 22.1% of women were never married. For non-Hispanic Black adults, the statistics were higher with 35.6% of Black men and 27.7% of Black women never being married in 1970.[187] And by 2020, the figures rose to 35.8% and 30% for all Americans, yet 51.4% of Black men and 47.5% of Black women were never married.[188] Let's look at some historical factors that contribute to these depressed Black marital statistics.

During Antebellum slavery, Blacks, labeled as property, were unrecognized as God's-image-bearers to slave owners and therefore did not receive the right to enter into any legal civil contract, such as marriage. Nevertheless, many enslaved couples lived together as husband and wife after undertaking wedding celebrations, such as jumping over a broomstick or throwing a grand feast for the entire community upon a man and woman professing their love and commitment to one another.[189] Without legal civil contracts, Black couples

---

[186] "African Americans and Black Community." National Healthy Marriage Resource Center. http://www.healthymarriageinfo.org/research-policy/marriage-facts-and-research/marriage-and-divorce-statistics-by-culture/african-americans-and-black-community/ (accessed September 29, 2022).

[187] Chanell Washington and Laquitta Walker, "Marriage Prevalence for Black Adults Varies by State," July 19, 2022. United States Census Bureau. https://www.census.gov/library/stories/2022/07/marriage-prevalence-for-black-adults-varies-by-state.html (accessed September 1, 2022).

[188] Chanell Washington and Laquitta Walker, "Marriage Prevalence for Black Adults Varies by State."

[189] Katherine M. Franke, "Becoming a Citizen: Reconstruction Era Regulation of African American Marriages," *Yale Journal of Law and the Humanities*, 11.2 (1999): 252.

considered themselves married before the eyes of God, the community, and, in some cases, their owners.[190]

During the Reconstruction period, marriage became legal for African Americans and for those unmarried; strengthening the Black family unit through marriage became vital. Marital laws and norms afforded Black people social and economic benefits previously foreclosed to them but on the condition that Black people abide by the race- and gender-based rules of conformist culture. *Tenancy and African American Marriage in the Postbellum South* by Deirdre Bloom and Christopher Muller shows that the racist tenant-farming economy of the Reconstruction era increased the incidence of both marriage and divorce among Blacks. We suggest that this unfortunate chapter in the history of Black American marriage soured future generations of Black folks toward marriage. African Americans who emerged from slavery were forced to be the kinds of citizens that Southern society depended upon at that time.[191] The association of marriage with tenant farming as a form of subjugation gave marriage a bad name in the Black community.[192] Since many African Americans did not enter into legal civil marriages on their own terms or using their own values, this bred animosity toward marriage for many Black people[193]. Nonnegotiable terms were set by the white-dominant culture to control how the Black family functioned. For example, in the postbellum South, numerous African Americans had no choice but to hold to their former enslavement socioeconomic conditions due to many white landowners refusing to sell land to African Americans and preventing Black families to generate wealth independently. Black women were forced into marriage in order to survive because southern counties presented tenant farming as the main means to earn income *but*

---

[190] Ibid., 252.
[191] Ibid., 252.
[192] Deirdre Bloome and Christopher Muller, "Tenancy and African American Marriage in the Postbellum South," *Demography*, 52.5 (2015):1409–30.
[193] Ibid., 3.

only for male-headed households.[194] This gender inequality resulted in many Black marriages dissolving.[195]

Since whites could no longer publicly display their abusive overseer ways, they required some Black husbands to *publicly* display similar harsh behavior toward their wives and children to farm the land[196]. Over time, Black marriage was tarnished by the money and power of white racists, as property owners' rights prevailed over Black human rights. These factors play a role in how some African Americans view marriage today.

Reflections on Contemporary Black Marriage

Today's Black-white marriage gap is best explained by labor market disparities and other structural disadvantages that Black people face, especially Black men.[197] One social change that has undermined Black marital rates today is a shift in the way some Blacks view marriage. The racial gap in marriage that emerged in the 1960s, and has grown since, is also partly due to broad changes in ideas about family arrangements that have made marriage *optional*. As the imperative to marry has fallen alongside other changes in the economy that have increased women's economic contributions to the household, socioeconomic standing has become increasingly important for marriage. Changes in attitudes concerning personal success, divorce, and premarital sex, with their growing acceptance, have encouraged Blacks to delay marriage and, in some cases, to cohabit outside of marriage.

Notwithstanding an increase in women's socioeconomic status, Black men and women still face a wealth gap relative to whites. Blacks

---

[194] Ibid., 2.
[195] Ibid., 2.
[196] Susan A. Mann, "Slavery, Sharecropping, and Sexual Inequality," *Signs*, 14.4 (1989): 773–87.
[197] R. Kelly Raley, Megan M. Sweeney, and Danielle Wondra, "The Growing Racial and Ethnic Divide in U.S. Marriage Patterns," *Future Child*, 25.2 (2015): 89–109.

read this wealth gap as a reason not to get married. Race continues to be associated with economic disadvantage, and as economic factors have become more relevant to marriage and marital stability, the racial gap in marriage has grown.[198] Marital stability and marriage formation are more strongly linked to the transition into stable employment for both men and women—hence Blacks' economic disadvantage becomes a greater destabilizing factor to marriage. Black families accumulate less wealth than white families. Additionally, young Black couples are less likely to have a nest egg to fall back on if they lose their jobs and are less likely to be able to rely on their parents for support during rough times.

Other factors associated with disparate marriage patterns between Black and white adults include an imbalanced gender ratio as well as high incarceration rates among Black males.[199] Mass incarceration of Black men reduces the pool of eligible bachelors available to Black women seeking Black husbands. Employment, wealth, and shifting views account for a sizeable portion of the contemporary racial gap in marriage.

Sankofa Marriage

In the face of shifting views of marriage, unrealistic standards perpetuated by popular culture, and racial and financial disparities, those in the African diaspora should nonetheless consider and persevere in lawful marriage. We must change the way in which Black marriage is viewed and pursued in order to advance the cause of equality and freedom.[200]

---

[198] R. Kelly Raley, Megan M. Sweeney, and Danielle Wondra, "The Growing Racial and Ethnic Divide in U.S. Marriage Patterns," 89–109.

[199] Chanell Washington and Laquitta Walker, "The New Great Migration and Black Marriage Trends in the South," April 7, 2022. United States Census Bureau. https://www.census.gov/library/working-papers/2022/demo/SEHSD-WP2022-07.html (accessed August 29, 2022). Kerwin Kofi Charles and Ming Ching Luoh, "Male Incarceration, the Marriage Market, and Female Outcomes," *The Review of Economics and Statistics*, 92.3 (2010): 614–627.

[200] Ibid., 309.

Black marriage as social justice prioritizes collective Black flourishing. A precedent for this communal emphasis is found in several African cultures. As a counterpoint to the antebellum history of Black marriage as a necessary adjustment to white supremacist structures, communal African marital traditions empower Black couples and communities. This cross-cultural perspective is helpful for promoting marriage among the African diaspora in the United States. Prior to European colonization, marriage was a norm in various parts of Africa. Monogamous, heterosexual marriage uniquely contributes and has contributed to African communities. To date, contrary to European marital norms of individualist contracts, African marriages have been driven by communal well-being.[201] For example, the preservation of family, clan, and culture is a driving factor for marriage in southern Nigerian life.[202] African marriage is more public than European marriage in that two different families are merging to become one new institution. Traditional African marriage is viewed as a covenant between two communities.[203] Among the Luo of Kenya, individuals marry on behalf of their communities and families.[204] Marriage is seen as a social duty, not an individualized pursuit. Due to the high group culture in many parts of Africa, a man and a woman embarking upon marriage honor particular physical, religious, and economic obligations.[205] If a woman's husband dies, then that woman will be taken care of by her new family. The brother of the husband who died will step in and assume guardianship over the widowed wife.[206] Familial justice will never run out for that widowed woman, and this is

---

[201] James W. Welch, "Can Christian Marriage in Africa be African?" *International Review of Mission*, 22.1 (1933): 17–32.
[202] Ibid., 19.
[203] Otieno Ishmael Opiyo et al., "The Challenges of Christian Marriages in Contemporary Africa," *Impact: Journal of Transformation*, 4.1 (2021): 49.
[204] Ibid., 48.
[205] Welch, "Can Christian Marriage in Africa be African?" 24.
[206] Ibid., 23.

a custom seen within the Afro-Asiatic people followed in Scripture (Deut. 24:19, 25:5).

Historically, African communities have stressed the importance of marriage to their children. Young girls were closely attached to their grandmothers who trained them to be successful future wives. Likewise, young men were trained by their grandfathers on how to be responsible future husbands.[207] Precolonial African marriage allowed Africans to depend upon their families for physical and social survival. Black marriages in this country have started to adopt this collectivist ethos, which shaped others for the better. Since biblical and African marriage are communal and cultural, we suggest that marriage lends itself to social justice. Black marriage can benefit not only the married couple but their entire family, church, and communities around the world. The following case studies highlight the tradition of Black marriage empowering Black communities in the United States.

Case Studies of Black Marriages That Advanced Social Justice

Moses Grandy, who was born a slave in 1786 in North Carolina, later became an author and abolitionist who worked to improve the social condition of his wife and some of his children by purchasing their freedom from slavery. Due to slave trading, he never found his other children, though he did not stop searching for them until the day he died.[208]

In 1848, William and Ellen Craft escaped from the South to Philadelphia, and Ellen used her light skin to pass as a white woman enslaving her dark-skinned husband, William, in their pursuit of freedom.[209] Approximately 20 years after their escape from slavery, Ellen

---

[207] Otieno Ishmael Opiyo et al., "The Challenges of Christian Marriages in Contemporary Africa," 49.
[208] Moses Grandy, *Narrative of the Life of Moses Grandy, Late a Slave in the United States of America* (Chapel Hill, NC: UNC at Chapel Hill Library, 2011), 23–35.
[209] William Craft, *Running a Thousand Miles for Freedom: The Escape of William and Ellen Craft from Slavery* (Athens, GA: University of Georgia Press, 1999), 79.

and William contested for Black social progress by starting a farmers cooperative and two schools (one school for children and one for adults) that educated newly freed Blacks.[210]

In the 1950s and 60s, Medgar Evers and his wife Myrlie Evers fought for the desegregation of the University of Mississippi, voting rights, and the desegregation of public facilities.[211] Their commitment to social justice helped create equal footing for public education, business, and government for African Americans. Medgar's assassination in 1963 galvanized President John F. Kennedy to ask Congress for a comprehensive civil rights bill, which President Lyndon Johnson signed into law the following year.[212]

These Black marriages and other Black married couples today that currently contest for social justice are the loci of the transmission of Christian values, which provide a social framework of inclusion for many underserved communities. But there is more work in which Black marriages must persevere.

A Practical Theology on Black Marriage as Social Justice

Black couples should marry and unite in various ways for Black social justice. Our practical theology on Black marriage as social justice posits four principles:

1. Unity — As led by God, African Americans should consider marrying one another. Unite. Black congenial company is able to sympathize with the pain caused by the injustices in this country. Although all of our experiences as Blacks in this country

---

[210] Eds. George Hendrick et al., *Fleeing for Freedom: Stories of the Underground Railroad as Told by Levi Coffin and William Still* (Chicago, IL: Ivan R. Dee, 2004), 22.
[211] Myrlie Evers Williams and William Peters, *For Us, the Living*, First edition (New York City, NY: Doubleday, 1967), 188, 251.
[212] "About Medgar and Myrlie." Medgar & Myrlie Evers Institute. https://eversinstitute.org/about-medgar-myrlie/ (accessed September 27, 2022).

are not identical, the vast majority of us have experienced some racial discrimination; we have been overlooked, discounted, and vilely disrespected. However, Black couples are able to identify and support each other in the face of injustice.[213] We can increase unity by advocating for our spouses and by providing a listening ear to increase understanding. Black couples can also unite to overcome external challenges to marriage together and minister to one another in both love and truth.

2. Foster and/or adopt Black children — Black married couples should consider socially oppressed Black children in the foster care system and look to foster or adopt Black children. Black children make up a disproportionate number of children identified as victims by child protective services and children waiting to be adopted.[214] Scripture instructs us to care for orphans.[215]

3. Ministry — Black married couples should be a light in a dark place and minister with our spouses to our neighbors (mentor and disciple other children from single-parent households, minister to the elderly and incarcerated). Live missionally to carry out the Great Commission.[216]

4. Stewardship — Black married couples should attend local zoning board meetings with their families and churches to fight against sophisticated contemporary forms of segregation

---

[213] Eccl 4:9–10.
[214] "Disproportionality and Race Equity in Child Welfare," January 26, 2021. National Conference of State Legislatures. https://www.ncsl.org/human-services/disproportionality-and-race-equity-in-child-welfare (accessed October 15, 2022).
[215] Jas 1:27.
[216] Matt. 28:19–20.

in our cities.²¹⁷ Let us pursue entrepreneurial and philanthropic efforts to support the next generation—fighting for social justice is fighting to gain financial wealth so that the next generation isn't suffering from a deficit. Let us take advantage of the tax and financial benefits of marriage to eliminate unhelpful debt and invest wisely in ministry and in the economy.

Following such tenets can help build loving partnerships and mutual respect between Black husbands and wives that benefit us all socially.

Black marriages have proven to be a vehicle of God's grace by shaping families, benefiting local U.S., as well as global, communities to administer the social justice God intended. Black marriage has improved socioeconomic status, helped many underserved communities, provided mental and emotional support, and proven to shape children positively in many households. Black marriage and social justice can intersect in ways that holistically empower individuals, couples, and communities. Black marriage can help to fill communal social justice gaps, advance the gospel of Jesus Christ in word and deed, and change the trajectory of our people.

---

²¹⁷ "For us in the racial world, the remade world, a crucial point of discipleship is precisely global real estate. Where we live determines in great measure how we live. Where we agree to the spatial configurations of land inevitably means a tacit agreement to the racial formation of the world. We must enter the struggle of land acquisition, space and place design, targeted housing development, buying, and selling which constantly reestablishes and strengthens segregationist mentalities and racial identities. We must, for example, disrupt the smooth formation of global real estate brokers and entrepreneurs formed in a process that deepens the logic of displacement and tightens the connection of space to commodity form, yielding the further naturalization of distinct living spaces for peoples with varying degrees of capital." Willie James Jennings, *The Christian Imagination: Theology and the Origins of Race* (New Haven, CT: Yale University Press, 2010), 287.

Developing a Pastoral Response to Racial Trauma

Melanie Taylor

Introduction: The Condition

In 2018, *The New York Times* featured a story entitled "A Quiet Exodus: Why Black Worshippers are Leaving White Evangelical Churches.[218]" Campbell Robertson chronicled the pent-up thoughts and emotions of Black Christians who had languished for years in white evangelical spaces to be later devastated by the outcome of the 2016 presidential election.[219] This particular story, and the experiences it covered, became fodder for robust debate among Black Christians. Leaders took note of the number of Black Christians immersed in or leaving majority-white spaces, whether workplaces or churches. Some responded with exegetical reminders of the enduring multiethnic nature of the global Christian Church, admonishing Black Christians to "hold on just a little while longer"; they maintained that our long-term ministries may be to reform these white Christian institutions from the inside. Others admonished Black believers to invest their spiritual gifts and zeal into building their own fellowships and

---

[218] Campbell Robertson, "A Quiet Exodus: Why Black Worshippers Are Leaving White Evangelical Churches," March 9, 2018. *The New York Times*. https://www.nytimes.com/2018/03/09/us/blacks-evangelical-churches.html.
[219] Robertson, "A Quiet Exodus," 2018.

institutions apart from the interests—and hindrances—of whiteness. Many Black Christians today, however, find themselves somewhere between the two poles, unsure of what staying or leaving might mean for them.

The quiet exodus in the late 2010s was later followed by racial upheaval and a global pandemic in 2020. Healthcare inequity, police brutality, prosecutorial injustices, and the impacts of poverty have loomed large. Widespread shutdowns created a margin to acknowledge many of the traumas that Black Christians have carried since our ancestors first arrived on this land—whether they came forcibly or voluntarily. Counselor and spiritual director Sheila Wise Rowe defines racial trauma, in particular, as:

> the physical and psychological symptoms that people of color often experience after a stressful racist incident. These personal or vicarious incidents happen repeatedly, causing our racial trauma to accumulate, which contributes to a more insidious, chronic stress.[220]

Racial trauma can result from racism in any form, including interpersonal, systemic, spacial, environmental, white privilege, internalized, defensive othering, or any combination thereof.[221] Within Black communities, we often feel compelled to suffer in silence or choose which issue to address to the neglect of all others. There is a myriad of reasons for this, not the least of which being the breadth and severity of traumas suffered by previous generations.

Black parents in America have often made the excruciating choice to send their own children into harm's way in pursuit of better opportunities. Some Blacks have assumed responsibility for not only integrating white institutions but changing "hearts and minds"

---
[220] Sheila Wise Rowe, *Healing Racial Trauma: The Road to Resilience* (Downers Grove, IL: IVP, 2020), 10.
[221] Rowe, *Healing Racial Trauma*, 6–9.

along the way. We reap the benefits of these intergenerational sacrifices today. But integration into white space has also necessitated and produced interpersonal skills like "biculturality" among many Black Americans.[222] This biculturality comes with trade-offs, engendering a "double-consciousness" in some.[223] W.E.B. Du Bois describes life for Blacks in the American context.

> This American world [is] a world which… only lets him see himself through the revelation of the other world. It is a peculiar sensation, this double-consciousness, this sense of always looking at one's self through the eyes of others, of measuring one's soul by the tape of a world that looks on in amused contempt and pity. One ever feels his twoness—an American, a Negro; two souls, two thoughts, two unreconciled strivings; two warring ideals in one dark body, whose dogged strength alone keeps it from being torn asunder.[224]

The benefits of integration have not been reaped without significant traumas. There are similar testimonies of mental, emotional, and spiritual harm amid the "quiet exodus" from white evangelical churches and other institutions.[225]

Being one of a handful of Black Christians in a ministry setting often comes with an unwritten set of expectations. One may feel as though the responsibility to move the ministry toward racial justice and reconciliation rests squarely on their shoulders. At the same time, Black Christians often receive both overt and subtle messaging from whites, "Be stereotyped, don't go too far, don't shatter our illusions

---

[222] Beverly Daniel Tatum, *Why Are All the Black Kids Sitting Together in the Cafeteria?: And Other Conversations About Race* (New York, NY: Basic Books, 1997), 13–14.
[223] W.E.B. Du Bois, *The Souls of Black Folk* (New York, NY: Simon & Schuster Paperbacks, 2009), 7.
[224] DuBois, *The Souls of Black Folk*, 7.
[225] Robertson, "A Quiet Exodus," 2018.

about you, don't amuse us too seriously. We will pay you."[226] Despite the fact that Black Christians did not establish systemic racism, the onus to reform white church structures can fall squarely on our shoulders even as we are crushed under its weight. Of course, there is an overarching oneness in the body of Christ that we do well to attend to, including bearing one another's burdens.[227] However, we succumb to utilitarian overlays of Western culture by overidentifying with the need to reform white spaces. This does not mean that *some* Black Christians will not have race-focused ministries in white spaces to the glory of God. But this is not the foremost calling for Black Christians, wholesale.[228]

It is far too easy for Black Christians in white spaces to fall into an embodied state of double-consciousness. This is a state in which we see our *primary* value as meeting the needs of white Christians—to answer their questions, to be their entry point into another culture, to assuage their guilt. We may struggle under this mantle at length out of care and concern for other Black Christians in our and similar contexts. Addressing white ignorance and racism is necessary and can eventually create an environment more conducive to Black flourishing.

---

[226] Langston Hughes, "The Negro Artist and the Racial Mountain," Poetry Foundation. https://www.poetryfoundation.org/articles/69395/the-negro-artist-and-the-racial-mountain (accessed October 20, 2022).

[227] Gal. 6:2

[228] I am guided here by the words of the great American author Toni Morrison from her address at Portland State University on May 30, 1975: "…the very serious function of racism [is] distraction. It keeps you from doing your work. It keeps you explaining over and over again, your reason for being. Somebody says you have no language and so you spend 20 years proving that you do. Somebody says your head isn't shaped properly so you have scientists working on the fact that it is. Somebody says that you have no art so you dredge that up. Somebody says that you have no kingdoms and so you dredge that up. None of that is necessary. There will always be one more thing.… And I urge you to be careful. For there is a deadly prison: the prison that is erected when one spends one's life fighting phantoms, concentrating on myths, and explaining over and over to the conqueror your language, your lifestyle, your history, your habits. And you don't have to do it anymore. You can go ahead and talk straight to me." Toni Morrison, "A Humanist View," Speech at Portland State University, May 30, 1975. https://www.mackenzian.com/wp-content/uploads/2014/07/Transcript_PortlandState_TMorrison.pdf.

But an embodied state of double-consciousness is, in itself, trauma-inducing. It can lead to painful cultural isolation and the conflating of one's self-worth with white Christians' willingness, or lack thereof, to repent of racism.

The Role of Pastoral Caregivers

The Black Church has often been accused of stigmatizing seeking psychological care. At times, unfortunately, some pastoral caregivers have mischaracterized seeking mental healthcare outside of the church as evidence of a lack of faith. It is important to examine the root of this impulse. Anti-Blackness is insidious, if not doubly so for Black people struggling with their mental health. The American healthcare system itself is yet another system corrupted by racism and prejudice. Physicians sworn to "first, do no harm" have been purveyors of some of the grossest acts of abuse in American history. In 1851, Dr. Samuel Cartwright, a white man, coined the term "drapetomania" to name a disease he believed was plaguing enslaved Black people. Dr. Cartwright surmised that it was this disease that caused the enslaved to flee their captivity. Believing that slavery was normative and even beneficial for Black people, he concluded that mental illness had to be the factor compelling them to run away.[229] With a legacy like this, it follows that Black Americans might hesitate to trust that psychological caregivers have their best interests in mind.

Many Black Christians turn to their pastoral caregivers as sources of understanding and healing from racial trauma. Some may need clinical intervention, but those resources are not always available or accessible to Black communities.[230] Others may be suspicious of for-

---

[229] Samuel A. Cartwright, "Diseases and Peculiarities of the Negro Race," Africans in America, PBS. https://www.pbs.org/wgbh/aia/part4/4h3106t.html (accessed May 18, 2023).
[230] Daniel Bolger and Pamela J. Prickett, "Where Would You Go? Race, Religion, and the Limits of Pastor Mental Health Care in Black and Latino Congregations," *Religions*, 12.12 (2021): 2–3, 8.

mal therapy or uncomfortable pursuing it. Regardless of one's access to mental health professionals, there remains a great need to address the spiritual impact of racial trauma beyond disembodied quoting of Scripture or an isolated prayer life. We can draw applicable principles from God's calling of Moses in Exodus to craft a biblically informed, Spirit-led, and psychologically sensitive pastoral response to racial trauma.

A Wilderness Respite: Discerning the Spirit's Invitation

In Exodus, the Hebrew people are dwelling in a land not their own. Exodus 1:9–10 tells us that the Pharaoh enslaved the Hebrews because he feared they would grow to outnumber the Egyptians, form alliances with political enemies, and eventually leave Egypt. Egyptians simultaneously despised the Hebrews *and* did not want them to leave. Hebrew enslavement revolved around bolstering the empire that perpetuated their condition.

Similarly, enslaved Africans were brought to the Americas to do forced labor. The profit from the sale of Black bodies and the labor they produced propelled European nations—and the thirteen colonies—to global superpower status. Echoes of these capitalistic ethics have seeped into discipleship praxis. For example, capitalistic ethics can influence us to measure spiritual maturity purely in terms of productivity and statistical improvement—increased time spent engaged in spiritual disciplines, more ministry activity, financial contributions to just causes—rather than how we are developing in relationship to God. While external indicators can illuminate the Spirit's work, spiritual development does not occur in a continuous trajectory of improvement or maximization of outcomes. Black Christians must take care not to define their relationships to white spaces solely in terms of their productivity. This type of dynamic is not sustainable, nor is it conducive to healthy identity formation.

The Exodus narrative is one of identity formation for the Hebrew people. Scripture does not always provide much background information on its most well-known leaders, but Moses's story is rich in detail. God takes an intimate interest not simply in Moses's execution of tasks but in healing Moses's sense of identity and restoring his connection to the Hebrews. Moses is profoundly aware of his own liabilities during his burning bush encounter on Mount Horeb; he was not Egyptian enough for the Egyptians or Hebrew enough for the Hebrews, and he was a "foreigner" in Midian.[231] This perpetual lack of cultural belonging undoubtedly amounted to a measure of trauma. By the time of this interaction, there is considerable distance between Moses's present reality and his self-identification as a Hebrew. But God addresses Moses as *an enculturated person*—not simply a warm body available to perform a task. Being called by God, Moses responds with, "Who am I that I should go to Pharaoh and bring the Israelites out of Egypt?"[232] He is afraid, lacks confidence, and is encountering God for the first time in his memory. Moses is so far removed from his own heritage that he does not even know the name of the "God of the Hebrews"—his God, by heritage.[233] Rather than shaming Moses's lack of cultural and spiritual awareness, God shares a profound and intimate moment of revelation; God reveals the long-awaited deliverance of the Hebrews to Moses *first*, not to his older brother Aaron or to the Hebrew elders.

This burning bush moment is rich, as it reveals YHWH to indeed be a "Wonderful Counselor."[234] The repeated losses of family, place, and identity are likely traumatic for Moses, but God has used them to shape Moses into a pastoral liberator for the Hebrews. Moses is not simply commissioned as a liberator because he is available. God aims

---

[231] Ex. 2:14, 22.
[232] Ex. 3:11.
[233] Ex. 3:13.
[234] Is. 9:6.

to heal Moses's layered racial trauma in the process by restoring him to the Hebrews not just as a community member but to shepherd them to freedom. In the process of his obedience, Moses is reconciled to his own ethnic identity and positioned to bring about the deliverance he desired for his people. His pedigree is complex, but it is the assurance of God's presence that empowers Moses as a leader, bringing synergy to his life story for God's glory and to the benefit of others.

From Moses's story, we see that God engages our racial and ethnic backgrounds as integral aspects of our identity formation. Unfortunately, contemporary Christian rhetoric often engages race and ethnicity through a prism of desired outcomes; race and ethnicity, if engaged at all in evangelical spaces, might be leveraged as part of church growth or mission strategies while being neglected in spiritual formation. I propose a break from utilitarian engagement with these aspects of our identities. Black Christians often struggle to reconcile their faith in Jesus with the use of Scripture in perpetuating enslavement, colonialism, and anti-Black racism across the globe. The disillusionment cascading from these questions must be addressed in our spiritual formation.

Given the infanticide visited upon his people by the Egyptians, Moses may have been one of few Hebrew men his age living in Egypt. One can imagine this may have translated to a type of survivor's guilt for Moses, as he was spared a life of slavery when he was transracially adopted by Pharaoh's daughters and "educated in all the wisdom of the Egyptians."[235] Many Black Christians may have experienced jarring separations from kinship networks due to systemic racism and injustice. Abdication of one's ethnic heritage and familial ties has historically been part of the price of entry into American culture at large.[236] Acts 7 lends insight into Moses's state of mind living at the nexus of such a sharp sociological juxtaposition.

---

[235] Acts 7:21–22.
[236] Chanequa Walker-Barnes, *I Bring the Voices of My People: A Womanist Vision for Racial Reconciliation* (Grand Rapids, MI: Eerdmans, 2019), 137.

> When Moses was forty years old, he decided to visit his own people, the Israelites. He saw one of them being mistreated by an Egyptian, so he went to his defense and avenged him by killing the Egyptian. Moses thought that his own people would realize that God was using him to rescue them, but they did not.[237]

While Moses's life was spared by his adoption, his "moving on up" into Pharaoh's household drove a wedge between him and his people as he grew older. The Exodus account tells us, "Looking this way and that and seeing no one, he killed the Egyptian and hid him in the sand."[238] This was an act of retribution precisely because the Egyptian was oppressing someone Moses himself identified with—a Hebrew.[239] Moses's liberative actions are discovered and wholly rejected by Hebrew workers.[240] Pharaoh turns his anger against Moses and tries to kill him for the second time, so Moses flees to Midian.

Doubly rejected, Moses finds himself in the desert without any cultural connection. Jethro's daughters perceive that Moses is an Egyptian—not a Hebrew—perhaps due to his dress and mannerisms.[241] Moses finds shelter, this time in Midian, with another distinct people group.[242] He feels secure enough there to marry and raise a family but is still plagued by feelings of being a cultural outsider. Exodus 2:22 reads, "Zipporah gave birth to a son, and Moses named him Gershom, saying, 'I have become a foreigner in a foreign land.'" Moses tends sheep for forty years in the desert as God ministers to his longing for family and shapes his protective instincts. God's people were called up and out of Egypt to commune with God in the wilderness.[243]

---

[237] Acts 7:23–25
[238] Ex. 2:12
[239] Ex. 2:11–12
[240] Ex. 2:14; Acts 7:35–39
[241] Ex. 2:19
[242] Ex. 2:12–22
[243] The desert in Scripture often functions as a "thin place" where God is encountered more clearly than what might be possible at the center of an empire.

"Throughout Scripture and the history of the church, the desert has been a place of spiritual preparation, purification, and transformation."[244] While it is tempting to read forty years of wandering after slavery as a harsh and reactionary punishment from God, it was intended as a providence. God used this season to undo the damage caused by Egyptian cultural genocide and establish a new God-centered Hebrew identity in the desert. God intended to bring Israel out of bondage entirely, not just physically but spiritually, emotionally, and socially as well.

Not unlike the ancient Hebrews, Black Americans have incurred injuries as they have done their best to survive racism and prejudice. One hallmark of Black survival in America has been the development of Black institutions. Historically Black colleges and universities (HBCUs) were founded because of de jure school segregation. While recent college enrollment trends show a decline in new students overall, HBCUs are making headlines with record enrollments as young Black and Brown students are intentionally choosing them over predominantly white institutions.[245] Ascension through the ranks of white institutions has historically been lauded as a hallmark of "making it." While integration of previously all-white institutions has been a necessary part of American history, one might argue that a generational shift is occurring as Blacks are redefining success to include intentionally investing in Black institutions. After years of striving for respect and advancement amid the white gaze, we are decidedly affirming the inherent wealth and value present within our own communities. These are markers of healing.

Choosing Black spaces after extended time in white spaces can prove spiritually akin to a wilderness oasis. It is important to note that

---

[244] Peter Scazzero, *The Emotionally Healthy Leader: How transforming your inner life will deeply transform your church, team and the world* (Grand Rapids, MI: Zondervan, 2015), 135.
[245] Erica L. Green, "Why Students Are Choosing H.B.C.U.s: '4 Years Being Seen as Family,'" June 11, 2022. *The New York Times.* https://www.nytimes.com/2022/06/11/us/hbcu-enrollment-black-students.html

"safe spaces," including all-Black spaces, are not always an available option, nor are they necessarily a respite for those experiencing intersectional marginalization.[246] While Black spaces are not perfect, the racially traumatized should not be discouraged from seeking cultural respite even after generations away in white spaces. Ultimately, wherever we can find it, "Each of us needs to identify and protect a desert space with God…"[247] We can find our respective Midian, like Moses did, and create space for spiritual and cultural rest, connection, and refocus. Time in our desert should be as routine as a weekly Sabbath or sabbatical or more permanent like the desert mothers and fathers.

Biblically Informed: Spirit-Led

Responding pastorally to the racial trauma of others necessitates that we are first willing to engage our own racial trauma. The Spirit is active in this process. We see this illustrated in Exodus as God forms Moses through Moses's periodic engagement with his own ethnic identity. Despite his upbringing in Pharaoh's household, God repeatedly engages Moses *as a Hebrew*, saying, "I am the God of your father, the God of Abraham, the God of Isaac and the God of Jacob."[248] Renowned psychologist and educator Dr. Beverly Daniel Tatum has written extensively on racial and ethnic identity development.

> Racial identity development… refers to the process of defining for oneself the personal significance and social meaning of belonging to a particular racial group. The terms racial identity and ethnic identity are often used synonymously, though a distinction can be made between the two. An ethnic group is a socially defined group based on cultural criteria, such as language, customs, and shared history…. In the case of either

---
[246] Chanequa Walker-Barnes, *I Bring the Voices of My People*, 68.
[247] Scazzero, *The Emotionally Healthy Leader*, 134.
[248] Ex. 3:6

racial or ethnic identity, these identities remain most salient to individuals of racial or ethnic groups that have been historically disadvantaged or marginalized.[249]

The phrase "defining for oneself" is critical. While those in our immediate communities may have opinions regarding the personal significance and social meaning of our ethnic identities, it is important that we invest time to define these for ourselves. Throughout Scripture, God affirms racial and ethnic identities as good and highly relevant for our spiritual formation. Acts 17:26–27 tells us that God "…marked out [the nations'] appointed times in history and the boundaries of their lands. God did this so that they would seek him and perhaps reach out for him and find him, though he is not far from any one of us." Christians must actively engage their own identity development as a matter of pastoral necessity. We cannot lead others in this aspect of formation if we have not first begun our own journeys.

If God is calling us to leave a particular context, we risk overstaying our assignments when fear keeps us bound to what is either familiar or appears advantageous. The security of familiarity, of being unique in a cross-cultural space, or of abundant resources does not equate to calling.[250] God kept Moses through Egypt for a season, but he was never meant to stay there or to change Egypt from the inside out. While God may have us in a context for a season, we cannot be pacified by predictability or privilege in the midst of oppression.

Clergy and laypersons must develop pastoral responses to racial trauma to more adequately address the chronic pains within our communities of faith. This necessitates that pastoral caregivers remain awake to the Spirit's direction, as it will change over time. We must undergo our own individual trauma work as pastoral caregivers lest

---

[249] Daniel Tatum, *Why Are All the Black Kids Sitting Together in the Cafeteria?*, 16–17.
[250] It is worth acknowledging that minority status in majority spaces is alluring to some when it elicits distinction and special privileges. Still, this unique positioning does not necessarily equate to calling or true influence beyond tokenization.

we project our own callings or predilections onto our flocks. Doing so requires open-hearted engagement with our whole self, including the traumas we carry, in the safe company of trusted others.

Biblically Informed: Psychologically Sensitive

The Hebrews' 430 years of slavery in Egypt do not fade from memory immediately once they are beyond Egypt's borders.[251] They blame Moses and cry to return to Egypt at many points along their journey, most often when they are faced with adversity or mundane anxiety in the desert. These moments of emotional flooding distort their memory and cause them to remember slavery as a comfort.[252] At least in Egypt, they knew where they would live and what they would eat. Dr. Chanequa Walker-Barnes offers a sobering analysis of internalized racism:

> When people of color internalize the view that whiteness is superior to all other races (including their own), we call this internalized oppression.... internalized oppression is not an unusual occurrence or merely the "exception to the rule"; it is the rule. It is a universal phenomenon. It is not limited to childhood but extends throughout the life span. It is so ubiquitous that detecting and reconfiguring the ways in which we have internalized racism takes considerable, intentional effort.... It also means that we tend to pathologize our own cultures, blaming them for anything that we see as a shortcoming in ourselves, our families, or our institutions.[253]

---

[251] Ex. 12:40

[252] Social worker and cultural somatics expert Resmaa Menakem has done extensive work to highlight the reality that trauma decontextualized over generations becomes misinterpreted as culture. We commonly remember the newly emancipated Hebrews as complainers today, perhaps because of our disconnection from their generational trauma.
Resmaa Menakem, *My Grandmother's Hands: Racialized Trauma and the Pathway to Mending Our Hearts and Bodies* (Las Vegas, NV: Central Recovery Press. 2017), 39.

[253] Walker-Barnes, *I Bring the Voices of My People*, 71.

One such way of engaging our racial trauma is forgiving ourselves for past instances of "self-abandonment."[254] Dr. Thema Bryant, ordained minister and president-elect of the American Psychological Association, addresses this reality on *The Homecoming Podcast with Dr. Thema*. Black Christians emerging from white spaces may often question if they stayed too long or compromised too much before leaving. If they consider leaving, they may agonize over how long to stay and what signs God might provide to aid in their discernment process. While exiled in Midian, Moses may have wondered if he waited too long in Pharaoh's household before acting on behalf of the Hebrews. These questions weigh on Black Christians considerably and can function as an isolating barrier even in the midst of sacred space. Ultimately, they can only be answered by the individual and the Spirit together. Pastoral caregivers can accompany Black Christians asking these questions by considering the following recommendations.

Four Practical Recommendations for Pastoral Caregivers

Sabbath Support Structures

As media streams inundate listeners with stories of racialized oppression, many individuals are seeking contextualized ministry that acknowledges their angst and moral injuries.[255] We need to build support structures into our daily lives that help us to metabolize pain and trauma. Social media breaks, advocacy, therapy, exercise, hobbies, routine medical care, and lament are wellness practices that enable us to feel the full range of human emotions in response to injustice. Observing the commandment of the Sabbath rest testifies that God

---

[254] Thema Bryant (Host). (November 21, 2021) Addressing Self-Abandonment (125) [Audio podcast episode]. In *The Homecoming Podcast with Dr. Thema*.
[255] Walker-Barnes, *I Bring the Voices of My People*, 125–126.

is God, and we are not. We honor the image of God in us when we commit to our own holistic healing. Pastoral caregivers can support parishioners by modeling this type of rest for their communities.

Moreover, Black Christians can set aside protected spaces for themselves, even within white institutions. Support groups within congregations can provide much-needed refreshment and encouragement for the journey. The mutuality experienced in these groups can help individuals experience cultural rest. These can be spaces for lament as well as opportunities for joy and celebration that do not require explanation.

Prophetic and Pastoral Presence

Church leaders and laypersons alike must cultivate a depth of identity security so as to remain present to such trauma with empathy and solidarity rather than reactivity. In doing so, the Spirit may illuminate the biblical text in ways we could not have understood otherwise. Christians actively engaging in racial and ethnic identity development can function as a balm in a world devastated by racial injustice. By offering biblical, Spirit-led, and psychologically sensitive pastoral care, we stand in as representatives of the ever-present God who is "I AM."[256] This process of intentionally engaging racial trauma enables believers to minister to the needs of a diverse Church with prophetic and pastoral specificity.

Black life in America is beset with sin, as is all of life, but our ministry must deal with more than abstraction. Dr. Soong-Chan Rah has addressed the differences among cultures regarding their orientation to guilt and shame. While European cultures tend to experience guilt and African, Asian, and Latino/a cultures tend to have a more visceral experience of shame, many Black Christians are trained to

---

[256] Ex. 3:14

preach a gospel that speaks primarily to guilt over individual sin.[257] We must specifically consider how our ecclesial communities may be shaped by white normativity and respectability politics. We can imagine "new wineskins" for pastoral care that are uniquely responsive to the times we inhabit and the questions with which Black people are wrestling.[258] Our care needs to be expansive and include more than behavior modification and individualistic-sin-focused preaching. We must address lived realities and their impact, not just the concept of individual sin and guilt. Our preaching and pastoral care must also address the manifestations of racial trauma due to issues that impede Black flourishing—from somatizations in the form of chronic illnesses to workplace trauma.

For a people who have been historically denigrated, we must take care that we are not reinforcing internalized racism through our preaching and pastoral care. This can happen unintentionally when internalized racism masquerades as holiness. Black people are likely experiencing the weathering of racism and white supremacy throughout the week in countless insidious forms. When Moses's trauma-induced inferiority complex caused him to say, "Who am I?" to the God who called him, God responded with, "I will be with you," and "I AM WHO I AM."[259] At its best, Black preaching is an embodied and communal experience. But even still, you cannot preach someone's racial trauma away. We must move from preaching *at* to presence *with* those suffering from racial trauma. There is power in the Name and in faithful pastoral presence. One need not be ordained or lead a congregation to administer either.

---

[257] Soong-Chan Rah, *Many Colors: Cultural Intelligence for a Changing Church* (Chicago, IL: Moody Publishers, 2010), 92.
[258] Mark 2:18–22
[259] Ex. 3:11–14

Affirm Our African Heritages

To counter internalized racism, pastoral caregivers should routinely and ardently affirm Black culture and spiritual expressions without needing to contort them into Eurocentric frames. Our Black is indeed beautiful without unnecessary qualifiers. Further, Dr. Vince Bantu writes, "The Western, white cultural captivity of the church is the single greatest obstacle for people coming to faith in Christ."[260] Indeed even Black people with familial and personal ties to Christianity have departed to old, new, and remixed religious movements in search of spiritual healing and cultural belonging. Forms of indigenous African and Afro-diasporic spiritualities like Yoruba, Vodou, and Kemeticism are attractive because they unabashedly affirm Black identity and purport to offer connections to our heritages—over and against Western Christianity. We must take these systems seriously as they present viable spiritual alternatives to our communities. It can no longer be taken for granted that Black people, if religious, will be Christian by default. Pastoral caregivers must create space for the generations to bring their questions, doubts, and traumas to their ministries, or they *will* go elsewhere.

Professional Psychological and Psychiatric Care

Pastoral caregivers must humbly recognize when a community member's racial trauma is beyond their scope of care. In light of historical taboos associated with mental infirmity, ministers should overcommunicate the necessity of both preventive and acute psychological care. Churches and ministries should establish connections with local healthcare professionals when possible so as to make recommendations and referrals for psychological and psychiatric support. It is worth churches and ministries investing financially in making

---

[260] Vince Bantu, *A Multitude of All Peoples: Engaging Ancient Christianity's Global Identity* (Downers Grove, IL: IVP Academic, 2020), 225.

these services available at reduced or no cost to eliminate barriers to entry.[261]

Conclusion

Following his bodily resurrection, Jesus bid his terrified male disciples to draw nearer and place their hands in his wounds so that they might fully recognize him. These were the same men who fell asleep while he sweated blood during prayer in Gethsemane and scattered upon his unjust arrest.[262] Jesus's profound, painful, and intimate act of receiving the disciples ushered them into a new stage of faith.[263] It is a "severe mercy" that we can recognize one another—and Jesus himself—through the wounds of our trauma.[264] Pastoral caregivers must develop a praxis that takes seriously the racial trauma that our communities, and others, are suffering.

Black Christians must feel the freedom to bring their racial trauma and questions of identity to the Church without fear of reprisal or rejection. This does not mean we romanticize or minimize the impact of sin on us. Rather, we invite God to transform and galvanize us to bring about change in our communities. While healing will be spiritually productive, we know that God's concern is for our wholeness and communion with Spirit, self, others, and creation and not more rote or frenetic church-sanctioned activity. We are set free from utilitarian and capitalistic overlays and invited into life-giving relationships that engage our trauma without defining us by it.

---

[261] I have seen clinics offer free and reduced-cost vouchers to churches to encourage clergy to refer parishioners for necessary care.
[262] Lk. 22:39–46
[263] Jn. 20:19–31
[264] Theologian C.S. Lewis coined the phrase "severe mercy" in letters to his friend, Sheldon Vanauken. In Vanauken's memoir, *A Severe Mercy*, Vanauken describes how his young wife's untimely death caused him to grow deeper in his Christian faith. After Lewis's introduction to this notion, Vanauken describes his grief as "A mercy as severe as death, a severity as merciful as love."
Sheldon Vanauken, *A Severe Mercy* (New York, NY: HarperSanFrancisco, 1980), 210–211.

Church leaders and laypersons alike must cultivate deep identity security so as to remain present to such trauma with empathy and solidarity rather than reactivity. In doing so, the Spirit may illuminate the biblical text in ways we could not have understood otherwise. Christians actively engaging in racial and ethnic identity development can function as a balm in a world devastated by racial injustice. By offering biblically informed, Spirit-led, and psychologically sensitive pastoral care, we stand in as representatives of the ever-present God who is "I AM."[265] This process of intentionally engaging racial trauma enables believers to minister to the needs of a diverse church with prophetic and pastoral specificity.

---

[265] Ex. 3:14

The Haymanot of the Metaverse

Michael Schultz

Society has steadily moved from the analog world of the Gutenberg printing press and the large, room-sized computation devices from IBM to a digital online presence. This movement to digitization is culminating at the intersection of high-capacity processing, low-cost storage, and a pervasive and immersive online creation known as the "metaverse."

The Haymanot (theology) of the metaverse seeks to consider modern integration with and participation in this new space called the metaverse. I will offer a few ethical responses for those wrestling with the ramifications of the pervasiveness and intrusiveness of the metaverse in our social and digital life.

Metaverse is a portmanteau of the words "meta" (self-referential) and "universe" (the entirety of human experience). The term was first coined "in the sci-fi novel 'Snow Crash' by Neil Stephenson in 1992, where humans interact with one another during a three-dimensional virtual space as avatars by wearing a virtual reality headset."[266] It imagines an immersive world accessed by users all over the world using their computers, physically connected to a global network. At present, it refers to a digital environment that is accessed through virtual reality (VR) or augmented reality (AR) interfaces, usually gog-

---

[266] Sailor Cahill, "Virtual Reality is the Future," September 16, 2021. Medium. https://medium.com/@sailorcahill/virtual-reality-is-the-future-e240c3cfa57b (accessed October 12, 2022).

gles or glasses of some type, or by using a PC or mobile device that allows access into this new world. At present, this space is segmented, with the various creators having no interaction with each other. The ultimate or end goal is a single space that encompasses all the providers, and each user is able to bring their individual avatar (that self-identified digital you) and any purchased or acquired items into the various connected realities that encompass this metaverse.

Whether it is augmenting the real world by overlaying objects only observable using specialized eyewear, or by using a mobile device, or by placing the user within a 360-degree environment, humanity is at the beginning of a new paradigm of living. It has become a new way of communicating, a new way of exploring the human imagination. It is a new way of social interaction now fully able to be realized using technology. In this new world, all of our real-world activities are able to be replicated and even enhanced using the various tools, new physics, and resources available and conceptualized by either human or artificial intelligence.

The metaverse—the new promise of escapism, economic gain, and social comradery—eerily echoes the temptations that Jesus faced and that the Apostle John warned against, saying, "For all that is in the world—the desires of the flesh and the desires of the eyes and the pride of life—is not from the Father but is from the world."[267] It is one world or many worlds where you can be anything, be it an animal, plant, or a real or imagined lifeform. You can be any gender, any size, tall or short, have six eyes and four arms, go anywhere, do anything, and fulfill any desire.

I raise the question to parents and those who are called to the higher purpose of preaching and teaching the tenets of the Christian doctrines—not only the preachers and teachers amongst us but all those struggling to slow down the inevitable encroachment of certain parts of the digital world, the darker underbelly filled with trolls,

---

[267] 1 Jn. 2:16

perverts, and a litany of individuals under the full control of our spiritual enemy.

How are we to respond to this paradigm shift in our society and engage each other and our families to mitigate falling into the grips of this NEW world with traps for "the desires of the eyes," "the desires of the flesh," or the "pride of life"? What should be the theology of the metaverse; does it inherently stem from the individuals connected via an interface, or is it defined by the internal social dynamics? Is it based on the various ethical models that define the response to the environment or the individuals in our community or social circles? There is a myriad of ethical and moral considerations that are both philosophically and theologically pertinent to our discussion because of incidents of sexual violence, bullying, pornography, profanity, and other antisocial behaviors that are and will be prevalent in this new space. We will look at a few of the ethical and moral implications as the beginning of a larger discussion that extends into both our future and the futures of our children.

This concept of augmenting or changing the perspective of what we see visually is not a new concept. It was first introduced in 1838 by Sir Charles Wheatstone, who "outlined the concept of 'binocular vision,' where you combine two images — one for each eye — to make a 3D image... [leading] to the development of stereoscopes... [which] use the illusion of depth to create an image." [268] This was one of the early catalysts for the research and development of various technologies to create and interact with images either in an entirely new digital space called virtual reality (VR) or using specialized glasses or devices to add or augment items in the real world, referred to as augmented reality (AR). Another forerunner to the creation of the internet, Vannevar Bush conceived what would ultimately become the

---

[268] Bernard Marr, "A Short History Of The Metaverse," March 21, 2022. Forbes. https://www.forbes.com/sites/bernardmarr/2022/03/21/a-short-history-of-the-metaverse/?sh=268e9ed85968 (accessed January 12, 2023).

world wide web: "a hypothetical electromechanical device that would store all books, records, and communications, and mechanically link them together by keyword associations, rather than traditional mostly hierarchal storage model." This concept eventually led to the internet being as integral a part of our daily lives as the air we breathe and the water we drink; no part of our life is not currently affected by some portion of the internet and its by-products.

A once-hypothetical space, the metaverse is now beginning to be as ubiquitous as the smart TVs, smartphones, and smartwatches most of us have. Many of our children and our grandchildren are aware of the various companies now producing and marketing this type of technology. Large multinational companies such as Microsoft with their HoloLens, Google's AR glasses, and Facebook's Oculus Quest are but a few large technology companies producing entry points into this new digital space. Gaming companies like Nintendo and Niantic with their Pokémon Go augmented reality game, saw users racing all over the world to "capture" Pokémon characters placed in real-world locations but only visible through their mobile game. Not only gaming companies but almost every industry now has some form of virtual or interactive way of communicating, training, or interfacing with customers or employees. We are witnessing the rise of new industries and the shifting of economic wealth with the innovations seen in the financial markets, with cryptocurrency now allowing for commerce to take place in the digital and the real world. New terms like "blockchain," "NFTs," "cryptocurrency," and "metaverse" are now everyday parts of our lexicon. It is the natural progression of our collective societal journey—from the oral traditions to the printing press, from the first landline telephones to satellite and mobile phones. It is inevitable that we will one day be integrated with our technology and are seeing the replacement of human biological parts with digital creations. Today, it is heart valves and prosthetic limbs; tomorrow, it is new eyes, new hearts, and new lungs—every part of biological creation can be and will be replaceable.

Interaction with the new digital universe, our metaverse, will be as instinctual and normative as turning on the television or jumping into our cars for a trip to the grocery store or grabbing your cell phone to order food or ring a loved one. Completely immersive and completely ubiquitous, our interactions will no longer be marked with visual human-to-human communication but communicating with a raft of various imagined or real entities. More and more, it will become difficult to distinguish humans from machines, and the ethical and moral frameworks that guide our societal relationships will and are currently being reimagined and reworked to fit this new paradigm.

There were early indicators of this need for new ethical and moral standards, with one of the earliest attempts coming from Isaac Asimov, one of the most prolific science fiction writers and technology prophets in the 1940s. He introduced the concept of moral guidelines for the eventual creation of humanoid synthetic beings (e.g., Will Smith's *I, Robot*) and proffered what is called the Three Laws of Robotics that provided what is now an industry standard. These laws are now widely used for guiding the discussion on standards of ethical behavior in synthetic beings, artificial intelligence, and the modeling and framing of behavior in the digital sphere or metaverse.

The three laws state, "A robot may not injure a human being or, through inaction, allow a human being to come to harm"; "A robot must obey orders given it by human beings except where such orders would conflict with the First Law"; "A robot must protect its own existence as long as such protection does not conflict with the First or Second Law."[269] This early attempt at applying ethical considerations for the interaction between synthetic or digital creations and the real world occupied by humans is now at an inflection point with the manifestation of the metaverse and its anticipated realization and widespread deployment. Synthetic beings are being devel-

---

[269] "Three Laws of Robotics." Wikipedia. https://en.wikipedia.org/wiki/Three_Laws_of_Robotics (accessed January 12, 2023).

oped to the point of broad deployment, but currently, we are seeing wide deployment of artificial intelligence (AI) in the real world and, more specifically, in the digital space or metaverse. Call any large company and try to get hold of a human; most of those interactions now are completely AI-driven and are now integral to our daily life. Think Siri or Alexa.

Many studies have been conducted on the impact of artificial intelligence and social media on the physical and mental well-being of users, especially our teens. According to Mayo Clinic, a "2019 study of more than 6,500 12- to 15-year-olds in the U.S. found that those who spent more than three hours a day using social media might be at heightened risk for mental health problems… Because of teens' impulsive natures, experts suggest that teens who post content on social media are at risk of sharing intimate photos or highly personal stories. This can result in teens being bullied, harassed or even blackmailed."[270] I posit this to be just a micro indicator of what will be a more pervasive issue with the advent of a lifestyle; when the time spent in the digital space ranges from eight, 10, 12, or more hours each day. We anticipate there will be a correlated uptick in the instances of bullying and other antisocial behavior directly related to the time spent and the increased number of users filling this space. For the African American population, Pew research data indicates that "Some 86% of African Americans ages 18–29 are home broadband adopters, as are 88% of black college graduates and 91% of African Americans with an annual household income of $75,000 or more per year."[271] Additionally, research has shown that "44% of Americans have suffered

---

[270] Mayo Clinic Staff, "Teens and social media use: What's the impact?" February 26, 2022. Mayo Clinic. https://www.mayoclinic.org/healthy-lifestyle/tween-and-teen-health/in-depth/teens-and-social-media-use/art-20474437 (accessed January 12, 2023).

[271] Aaron Smith, "African Americans and Technology Use," January 6, 2014. Pew Research Center. https://www.pewresearch.org/internet/2014/01/06/african-americans-and-technology-use/ (accessed January 12, 2023).

online harassment, 15% physical threats, 12% sexual harassment and 12% have been stalked"[272]

As the price of entry decreases and adoption increases, those looking to escape the lived experience of our "Afrocentricity" will, unfortunately, find that the metaverse offers little respite from the trauma of real-world experiences of racism and its real-world effects on the physical personhood. Author Ta-Nehisi Coates speaks to this physical response by highlighting "that racism is a visceral experience, that it lodges brains, blocks airways, tips muscle, extracts organs, cracks bones, breaks teeth… the economics, the graphs, the charts, the regressions all land, with great violence, upon the body."[273]

The metaverse is a space devoid of the moral guardrails, the cultural norms, and morays that normally knit our various cultures into a cohesive human family—moral and ethical standards that serve to hold at bay the baser instincts often rejected by the larger social order under threat of ostracism, incarceration, and ultimately state-sanctioned death in the form of the death penalty. It will be incumbent on the creators and companies responsible for providing content, access, and other products and services for the metaverse to establish strong ethical guidelines with the aim to mitigate the replication of real-world antisocial behavior in the digital space. In addition, there is also the responsibility of the individuals or agents connected to the larger social strata that must be made to understand they are part of a larger community, one centered in the real world and then extending into the virtual space. "Each agent must contribute to a common body of knowledge that supports the creation of a shared community worldview (that is itself complete, coherent, and good) through which social institutions and their resulting policies might flourish within

---

[272] Enjinstarter, "The Ethics of the Metaverse," August 25, 2021. Medium. https://medium.com/enjinstarter/the-ethics-of-the-metaverse-b532143cd4ef (accessed January 12, 2023).
[273] Ta-Nehisi Coates, *Between the World and Me* (New York, NY: Penguin Random House, 2015).

the constraints of the essential core commonly held values (ethics, aesthetics, and religion)."[274] Without these shared community worldviews, what arises in the vacuum is what Angela Gorrell in her book *Always On* called "diminished humanness"; "the result of not seeing yourself or other people as full beings with minds, hearts, emotions, hopes, friends, families, reputation, struggles… believing what you say and do online or through a device is not the 'real' you… this fact creates an actual separation between the person and their world and actions, which gives them the sense that their words and actions can be distanced from whom they understand their 'self' to be." [275]

The battle for our souls and minds has expanded, and now we have an entirely new space in which we, the purveyors of the gospel, are critically needed to help those of African descent who wrestle with decolonization and navigating a societal minefield that looks to minimize our culture, obfuscate in response to our cries of institutional racism, and marginalize our lived truth when we attempt to reap the same economic rewards as the majority culture. What we and our children are finding in this new space is more of the same; a wild, wild west of corrupt language, corrupt behavior, corrupt imagery, and corrupt lifestyle choices that are antithetical to Christian "Ret'at" or orthodoxy. We are currently ascending to the top of the mountain and are faced with the same vision of the world in all its glory and splendor that Satan showed Jesus, telling him, "*All these I will give you*, if you fall down and worship me."[276] It is the underlying premise of the promise placed before us in this new space and the battle now raging for the hearts, minds, and eyes. The statement rings in the ears of those faced with historical and current subjugation along with economic depravity institutionalized by the majority culture. The foundation of the

---

[274] Eds. Michael Boylan and Wanda Teays, *Ethics in the AI, Technology, and Information Age* (Lanham, MD: Rowman & Littlefield Publishers, 2022).
[275] Angela Williams Gorrell, *Always On: Practicing Faith in a New Media Landscape* (Grand Rapids, MI: Baker Academic, 2019).
[276] Matt. 4:9

promise—a world of inclusivity, personal expression of oneself, and the outward expression of one's creative capacity—becomes more prominent and highlighted to those looking for the means to achieve that which was previously deemed unattainable.

We must take up a standard as we counsel against the trap that is the *"desires of the eyes."* As parents, we are constantly fighting the million-dollar focus groups and marketing arms of companies that see us and our children as potential consumers in which to establish habits and relationships with their products and services. Our eye gates are consistently being subjected to the black screen of a reality that is often devoid of the message of the gospel or convoluted by the distractions of multiple streams of information rife with the falsehoods of half-truths, "fake news," and targeted biological manipulation. "Media manipulation tactics include: planting and/or amplifying misinformation and disinformation using humans (troll armies, doxing, and bounties) or digital tools (bots); targeting journalists or public figures for social engineering (psychological manipulation); gaming trending and ranking algorithms, and coordinating action across multiple user accounts to force topics, keywords, or questions into the public conversation."[277] We saw an example of this with the release of internal Facebook (Meta) documents that revealed their algorithms specifically focused on human behavioral studies and ways to create a Pavlovian response in the users of their social media platform. If we, as adults, find it difficult to put down those devices, how much more so do the undeveloped brains of our pubescent sons and daughters? Each new video, each new game or movie provides an entry point for these players who inherently do not have our and our children's best interests at heart. Imagine what the repercussions will be when we are immersed within the environment for extended periods of each day.

---

[277] danah boyd et al., "Media Manipulation & Disinformation." Data & Society. https://datasociety.net/research/media-manipulation/?type=resourcerch%2Fmedia-manipulation%2F%3Ftype

The metaverse is the newest battlefield for product marketing and a prime location for covetous behavior. The Bible has remedies for us as we approach this new paradigm and watch as control is wrested from parents unable to keep up with the various technological developments that are outstripping their knowledge and abilities to monitor. The book of John councils to love not the world or things of the world because the world has no intention of easing up, giving them a pass, or providing the means by which we can reassert control over the steady diet of "stuff" they are being force-fed daily, hourly, minute by minute, as their eyes are locked on their screens.

Within the metaverse, we are faced with the ever-present marketing arms of multinational companies who have spent billions on ensuring that the products and services being peddled are seen, heard, and ultimately, physically experienced. Christians recall the interaction between Jesus and the rich young man. Jesus asked him about his moral and ethical behavior, about loving and honoring his parents, not killing, not lying, or stealing. Lastly, we see Jesus getting to the core of his and many of our current and future issues. "If you would be perfect, go, sell what you possess and give to the poor, and you will have treasure in heaven; and come, follow me."[278] The response of the rich young man, unfortunately, was that "he went away sorrowful, for he had great possessions."[279]

This new "pride of life" is the promise of building your dream, be it a place of virtual residence or space to play in a new universe devoid of God's interference and the moral restraints that are institutionalized in various cultures. In this new world, you can mold the universe to suit your desires, and since it was NOT created by a sovereign God, the individual is placed there in his stead. We see an example of this self-glorification in the book of Daniel where King Nebuchadnezzar, looking out on the splendor of his palace, answered and said, "Is not

---

[278] Matt. 19:21
[279] Matt. 19:22

this great Babylon, which I have built by my mighty power... and for the glory of my majesty?"[280] The immediacy and severity of his judgment was informative of how God views this type of idolatry. We do not condemn the creativity and expression of artistic talent; what we attempt to guard against is the ease at which our own artistic talents can so easily turn to idolatry. We see this in the present culture where we find many of today's artists having started in a church context but fall victim to the trappings of the pull of the culture—be it for financial gain, popularity, notoriety, or other reasons (***the love of the world***). Most notable is one of our songstress Sister Whitney, a tragic example of a grounded beginning and a flawed ending. We reinforce the truths of God's desire to give us life more abundantly but not at the price of materialism and those things that are just pleasing to the eyes. It is easier said in this context when we are discussing the various obstacles and approaches. It is a difficult, real-life conversation with our sons and daughters faced with the pressures of peers, chemical changes to their bodies, and the constant barrage of a system that has been hammering away at their convictions, character, and moral foundation. We are living in a *ME* culture; one that was identified so long ago in scripture. We find this description in 2 Timothy, where it states that "in the last days there will come times of difficulty. For people will be lovers of self, lovers of money, proud, arrogant, abusive, disobedient to their parents, ungrateful, unholy, heartless, unappeasable, slanderous, without self-control, brutal, not loving good, treacherous, reckless, swollen with conceit, lovers of pleasure rather than lovers of God."[281]

The last and more pervasive and heinous trapping of the new metaverse is that which revolves around the lust of the flesh. These, brothers and sisters, are the areas that should keep us on our knees for our children and our friends, both male and female. As adults, we know

---

[280] Dan. 4:30
[281] 2 Tim. 3:1–4

the trappings of the internet and all that surrounds the underbelly of human depravity. The metaverse offers a more immersive option, and we are just at the beginning of what will be the most difficult battle yet to come. We know from Romans that we "all have turned aside; together [we] have become worthless, no one does good, not even one."[282] We have found secret worlds in Minecraft, a metaverse game for young children, where, in a secret section, the characters engage in all sorts of perversions. Grown men (and women) perpetrate deception, drawing young people into their web of deception and lies. There have been reports of places in some virtual worlds where, upon accessing, a young lady was sexually accosted within minutes of entry. We apply filters, monitor times, and attempt to monitor friends, who are being communicated with in some of these worlds, but we cannot be everywhere at all times. We pray to our Father in Heaven, who can be in all places, always, and sees all things and has asked the question, "Can a man hide himself in secret places so that I cannot see him?"[283] We answer with a resounding NO!

We thank our Lord, who does see when we can't, who does know when we do not, who does care when we've done all we can but have fallen short. We are "a chosen race, a royal priesthood, a holy nation, a people for his own possession, that you may proclaim the excellencies of him who called you out of darkness into his marvelous light."[284] We take that light and impart it early and deep within our children before we send them into a world that has only ill intent toward them, both in real and now the digital space.

African Americans or those who are part of the African diaspora—specifically in the Black Christian context—historically suffer from internalized trauma because of slavery, which is often manifested in self-defeating behavior. The outward expression of that trauma and its

---

[282] Rom. 3:12
[283] Jer. 23:24
[284] 1 Pet. 2:9

effects on the person are often mitigated by parental instructions based on biblical doctrines. Instructions and exhortations from the biblical text speak to a host of ethical and moral standards that are reinforced contextually. Although both the Old and New Testaments have varying points of view on the spectrum of human engagements, we must form a coherent foundation for our biblical worldview and impart that to our children and grandchildren.

When thinking about the theology of the metaverse, we can use the four Stoic virtues as a baseline to impose the ethical constructs needed to counteract the three main adversarial points raised: the desires of the eyes, the desires of the flesh, and the pride of life. The four Stoic ethical virtues are wisdom, justice, courage, and moderation. The first ethical standard, wisdom, should be cultivated by our interaction within this new space. We read that Solomon requests wisdom when the Lord appeared to him and said, "Ask what I shall give you."[285] This question elicits all three temptations as a potential response option. I want stuff, I want even more stuff, and I want to be the boss of everyone.

As we enter this new paradigm, as with any new space, the approach has to be with wisdom. First, establishing systems to monitor usage times and the conversations in chats provides transparency in where time is spent and what conversations are taking place. It also means limiting access and being cognizant of what mechanisms are in place on the various platforms that aid in reinforcing the routines and problematic conversations occurring.

The second standard is that of justice, one of the major attributes of God. This ethical position speaks to our duties to each other and the ways we interact with other users of the space. As noted in our comments about statistics of antisocial behavior, what we have seen is a diminished humanity in human interactions. The diminishing of humanity is not only in the interpersonal interactions but in

---

[285] 1 Kin. 3:5

the interactions with the host of AI-generated life forms. As the line between the real and the digital blurs, an established foundation of justice within the character helps to mitigate those behavioral patterns that may compromise real-world relationships. Principles like the statement in Amos 5:24, "let justice run down like waters, and righteousness like an ever-flowing stream," act as a moral line for anyone faced with decisions within this space that will ultimately call their character into question.

Next, we speak of the ethical principle of moderation in the metaverse—the principle of temperance or self-control. It is part of the fruit of the Spirit, as seen in the book of Galatians 5:22–23. Not being able to have control over oneself has led to the downfall of many (e.g., Saul, due to his many wives) and even to death, as seen in the example of Hophni and Phinehas in 1 Samuel 2:34. We stress self-control in the metaverse. The establishment of this core principle helps to safeguard the user and curtail any data breaches or privacy concerns.

Finally, we look at the ethical virtue of courage. Courage in the digital space is the ability to face the racism, harassment, and bullying that is prevalent. The Bible speaks to the virtue of courage in the face of the world system in scriptures such as Deut. 31:6: "Be strong and courageous. Do not fear or be in dread of them, for it is the Lord your God who goes with you. He will not leave you or forsake you." We know that the world and its desires are passing away, so we guard ourselves against real-world temptations, remembering that God is always present, even in the world of our creation.

In Psalm 139:7–8, David asked that rhetorical question that speaks to the inescapable truth of why the metaverse is not a place where we can escape the responsibility of our Christian walk or the ethical and moral standards we bring with us:

Where shall I go from your Spirit? Or where shall I flee from your presence? If I ascend to heaven; you are there! If I make my bed in Sheol, you are there!

Conclusion

In this paper, we have delved into the concept of the metaverse, a digital space that is becoming increasingly pervasive in our lives. We have explored the ethical and moral implications of engaging with this new realm and the challenges it poses to individuals, particularly those of African descent. The metaverse offers a seemingly limitless world of possibilities where individuals can be anything they desire, but it also presents dangers, such as the replication of real-world anti-social behavior, the promotion of materialism and self-glorification, and the potential for the exploitation and harm of users, especially young people.

As we navigate the metaverse, it is crucial to establish strong ethical guidelines and moral frameworks. The four Stoic virtues provide a useful baseline for approaching this new space. Wisdom reminds us to make informed decisions, seek knowledge, and set boundaries for usage. Justice calls us to treat others with fairness and respect, fostering healthy interactions and relationships. Temperance encourages self-control, guarding against the dangers of excess and addictive behavior. Finally, courage is essential to face the challenges of the metaverse, standing against racism, harassment, and bullying while maintaining our Christian values and integrity.

As parents, educators, and individuals called to guide and teach, we have a responsibility to impart these ethical principles and instill a strong biblical foundation in our children and communities. The metaverse may promise escape, economic gain, and social camaraderie, but we must not be swayed by its allure. Instead, we should approach this new paradigm with discernment, understanding the potential risks and striving to protect ourselves and others from its negative influences.

In conclusion, the theology of the metaverse requires us to navigate the intersection of faith, technology, and ethics. It calls for a deliberate and conscious effort to uphold our Christian values, promote justice and respect, exercise self-control, and demonstrate courage in the face of adversity. By doing so, we can participate in this new digital world while remaining grounded in our moral and ethical principles, ultimately shaping the metaverse into a space that reflects God's love and righteousness.

Is There a Word From the Lord? A Black Ecclesial Orthodox Theology of Preaching

Watson Jones III

During the 1975 Lyman Beecher Lecture series, Gardner Taylor impressed upon attendees the seriousness of preaching. For Taylor, preaching is not merely human-to-human discourse but a sacred moment where one speaks a message from God to people.

He says:

> Measured by almost any gauge, preaching is a presumptuous business. If the undertaking does not have some sanctions beyond human reckoning, then it is indeed rash and audacious for one person to dare to stand up before or among other people and declare that he or she brings from the eternal God a message for those who listen which involves issues nothing less than those of life and death. [286]

The task of preaching is audacious because a man or woman has the job of standing before people to declare, "Thus says the Lord." Taylor says God's speaking has life-or-death significance. Just as a

---

[286] Gardner C. Taylor, *How Shall They Preach: The Lyman Beecher Lecture and Five Lenten Sermons* (Elgin, IL: Progressive Baptist Publishing House, 1977), 24.

doctor takes special care when working with a patient, a preacher must reckon with the reality that he or she delivers words with great eternal weight.

While preaching is presumptuous, the task is never done in a vacuum. Instead, it always arises from the depths of one's core conviction and theological location. In other words, there are theological assumptions made in preaching. In this paper, I will present my theology of preaching from the perspective of my theological family—the Black Ecclesial Orthodox Tradition. I posit that my theological position is held by most of those who stand at the pulpit and sit in the pews of African American churches. Unfortunately, my theological family has primarily been underrepresented, marginalized, and mischaracterized in the academic discourse for far too long. Some have proffered definitions and descriptions to explain the theology and preaching of Black people. However, given what I believe to be the prevalence of those in the Black Church who hold similar convictions as myself, it is time for the voices of those in the Black Ecclesial Orthodox Tradition to be heard. I hope to voice the theological beliefs that underpin the Black Ecclesial Orthodox Tradition of preaching to raise a conversational partnership with other existing theological families in academia.

I will discuss my theology of preaching from the perspective of the Black Ecclesial Orthodox Tradition. To achieve this, I will define a theology of preaching, the components of a theology of preaching, and how that theology should guide preaching. Next, I will discuss the theological features that I deem most critical to a Black Ecclesial Orthodox theology of preaching. While the list could be longer, constraints cause me to name the essential elements. They are the Bible and preaching, the Gospel and preaching, the relationship between the preacher and the pew, and the goal of preaching.

Esau McCaulley, in his seminal work *Reading While Black,* argues that in the academy, the voices that comprise much of the

Black Church are left out of academic discourse altogether.[287] Instead, McCaulley suggests Black progressive voices have been mainly proffered by white progressives and used to "[depict] them as the totality of the Black Christian tradition for reasons that suit their purposes."[288] McCaulley's words resonate because we tend to feel like we are misfits. As a result, we in the Black Ecclesial Orthodoxy face criticism on every side; white conservatives criticize people in my theological tribe for being "too liberal," white progressives for being "fundamentalist," and Black progressives for being "too whitewashed" or simply lacking theological sophistication that, in their view, should lead to progressivism.[289]

Considering scholarly discourse, the focus of Black preaching tends to skew primarily toward liberation. For example, in *Methodologies of Black Theology*, Fredrick Ware notes, "Academic black theology (I add homiletics) is in a position of competition among oral traditions of black theology in African American churches and communities."[290] Cecil Cone and others criticized James Cone for similar reasons.[291] Much of the discourse around what constitutes Black Theology or preaching does not consider the embedded theologies in the average sermon from a Black pulpit. To be clear, the Black Church, and her pulpit, is not a monolith. Liberation is undoubtedly a theme in Black preaching, but it is not the only one.

McCaulley calls my theological tribe the "Black ecclesial interpreters."[292] He says we are "Black scholars and pastors formed by the faith found in the foundational and ongoing doctrinal commitments, sermons, public witness, and ethos of the Black church."[293]

---

[287] Esau McCaulley, *Reading While Black: African American Biblical Interpretation as an Exercise in Hope* (Downers Grove, IL: IVP Academic, 2020), 4.
[288] Ibid., 6.
[289] Ibid., 5.
[290] Fredrick L. Ware, *Methodologies of Black Theology* (Eugene, OR: Wipf & Stock, 2002), 27.
[291] Ibid., 14.
[292] McCaulley, *Reading While Black*, 4.
[293] Ibid., 4–5.

Therefore, in identifying the theological location of my preaching, I would label myself as a "Black Ecclesial Orthodox Traditionalist" or "Black Orthodox." We hold to theological orthodoxy (classical Christianity). Still, we are fiercely committed to "public advocacy for justice, its affirmation of the worth of Black bodies and souls, its vision of a multiethnic community of faith" in preaching and practice.[294]

Vince Bantu, in his seminal work *Gospel Haymanot*, refers to those of my theological tribe as "Gospelist."[295] In his work, he connects the Christians of the Black diaspora with the beliefs of African Christians who held to what Ethiopian Christian literature calls *haymanot rete't* or "right faith."[296] By right faith, he means orthodox Christian belief as passed down through the millennia, including high "biblical teaching and justice for the oppressed."[297] This is the Christianity that most Black Christians practice. It is a high view of the authority of Scripture as the Word of God, the exclusivity of the Gospel of Jesus, and an unwavering belief in a holistic gospel that reconciles people to God through Jesus and that "disrupts systems of injustice."[298]

For the Black Ecclesial Orthodox Tradition, preaching stands unwaveringly on the authority of Scripture. The Bible should be the basis and backbone of the sermon, instructing the congregation on what the Lord is saying. Since Black Christians embrace the Bible as the Word of God, God speaks to God's people in a biblical sermon. Secondly, in the Black Ecclesial Orthodox Tradition, the Gospel is proclaimed to call individuals to repentance and faith in Jesus and address the corporate sin of society.

---

[294] Ibid., 6.
[295] Vince L. Bantu, "An Introduction to Gospel Haymanot," *Gospel Haymanot: A Constructive Theology and Critical Reflection on African and Diasporic Christianity*, ed. Vince L. Bantu (Chicago, IL: Urban Ministry, Inc., 2020), 23.
[296] Ibid., 12.
[297] Ibid.
[298] Ibid., 23.

Theology of Preaching

If preaching is such a serious undertaking, one might ask, "What, then, is preaching?" Whereas a homiletical theory describes the "how" of preaching, a theology of preaching starts with a definition of what preaching is, moves to the theological assumptions made in preaching, and finally addresses the end goal of preaching.

What Is Preaching?

In the Black Ecclesial Orthodox Tradition of preaching, God speaking to people through the proclamation of the Gospel from the scriptures is essential. Therefore, I define preaching as *the proclamation* of the *Word of God* (God speaking) expounding on *God's inspired written text* (the Scriptures) as the *Holy Spirit equips* through the agency of a *preacher* to *people* at a *point in time* for a specific *purpose*. That is, God speaks through the proclamation of a preacher from a biblical text.

Olin Moyd says of the role of the preacher, "The audacious assignment is to speak for God and about God to the people of God of whom the preacher is just one called out as proclaimer."[299] This is essential in the Black Ecclesial Orthodox view of preaching and harkens to the question raised by the Black preaching in the preaching moment: "Is there a word from the Lord?" When the preacher raises that question, he or she recognizes the significance of that moment. God indeed desires to speak to God's people, calling them to repentance or strengthening them to push against and through the struggles of life.

In my view of the Black Ecclesial Orthodox view of preaching, one gauges God's speech from the scriptures, which are the backbone of the sermon. It is a proclamation *from* the Bible, considering what God has said in a text to its original audience, and considering what

---

[299] Olin P. Moyd, *The Sacred Art: Preaching and Theology in the African American Tradition* (King of Prussia, PA: Judson Press, 1995), 56.

God now has to say from that text to today's audience. Samuel Proctor viewed preaching as something more profound than merely reciting Scripture. He argues it is a "proclamation of the truth of God, through Jesus Christ, by a preacher endowed with spiritual discipline. The proclamation, informed by the Scriptures, relates to all of life."[300] We are given the scriptures as God's Word with the task of preaching from it that God's people might hear God speak to them in this present age and that they might know how to live.

Components of a Theology of Preaching

I will discuss the theological beliefs germane to my understanding of preaching: my view on the Bible and its relationship to preaching, the nature of the Gospel, the role and relationship of the preacher with the congregation, and finally, the purpose of preaching.

The Bible and Preaching

In discussing a theology of preaching, one has to grapple with the role and authority of Scripture in the sermon. The Bible is paramount to the sermon for those in the Black Ecclesial Orthodox view of preaching. Sermons that are not linked to the scriptures are often found wanting. The connection between the Bible and the sermon is the underlying assumption and presupposition one has about the Bible: the Bible is the *written* Word of God.

Some homileticians would argue differently from my position. Many opposing views are reactions against the caricatured image of the fundamentalist, where preaching does not undergo proper hermeneutics to interpret the text for responsible application. In the Black Ecclesial Orthodox Tradition, the preacher considers the corpus of Scripture, what we ascertain about God from them, and the Gospel of

---

[300] Samuel D. Proctor, *The Certain Sound of the Trumpet: Crafting a Sermon of Authority* (King of Prussia, PA: Judson Press, 1994), 9.

Jesus as presented in the Scripture. Like a tree in an immense forest, a particular text's meaning is always interpreted in the context of the whole Bible with the help of the Holy Spirit.

One ought not label the Black Ecclesial Orthodox as fundamentalist. The American fundamentalism movement is a response to the European enlightenment-influenced modernist critique of Scripture. However, for Black people, the orthodox position predates the fundamentalist/modernist debate and, as Thomas Oden says, "is transcendent" in that it ties closely to the beliefs of ancient African Christianity.[301]

Unlike fundamentalists, the Black Ecclesial Orthodox preacher approaches the Scripture not from a place of Bible-idolatry but one of high regard for the scriptures so that the preacher might bring grace and hope to the congregation from its text. Cleophus LaRue rightly asserts, "Unlike many who claim a deep-seated love for the Bible, blacks have typically not made the mistake of worshiping the Bible. They have, however, sought in their preaching and teaching to probe the unsearchable riches of God's grace as they are witnessed to and attested in the Bible."[302] The preacher understands that a listening congregation enters the preaching moment facing difficulties from oppression, existential concerns, and life struggles. The scriptures have something to say to them. The biblical text is where the preacher finds grace that helps the listening congregation.

Also, the Bible in the preaching moment is how Black preachers hear the disclosures of the Spirit; the "Living Word leaping up out of the *words* of the Scriptures (italics added)."[303] For the Black preacher, the words of scripture matter as the Word of God. Those words reveal to us the heart of the Living Word—Jesus. Since the Bible helps us

---

[301] Thomas C. Oden, *How Africa Shaped the Christian Mind: Rediscovering the African Seedbed of Western Christianity* (Downers Grove, IL: IVP Books, 2010), 129.
[302] Cleophus J. LaRue, *I Believe I'll Testify: The Art of African American Preaching* (Louisville, KY: Westminster John Knox Press, 2011), 59.
[303] Taylor, *How Shall They Preach*, 59.

see and *hear* Jesus, the preacher searches the written Word of God so that Jesus might confront the congregation. This divine confrontation then calls forth a life-altering and transformational response to Jesus.

The Gospel and Preaching

As one considers a theology of preaching, the next logical issue one must address is the content or message of a sermon—the Gospel. In the Black Ecclesial Orthodox perspective, the Gospel is a message that has personal and social implications. It addresses humanity's relationship with God and how humans relate to one another. The Gospel we preach is holistic because it highlights the atonement's penal significance and represents an otherworldly Kingdom that the incarnation and the resurrection bear witness to.

While the Gospel entails the incarnation of Christ, His life and teachings, and the new dawn of a new kingdom, the central element of the Gospel in the Black Ecclesial Orthodox position is the death of Jesus to pay for human sins and Christ's subsequent resurrection. Scholars like James Kay say that the Gospel is focused primarily on the cross and resurrection of Jesus Christ and is the announcement of the destiny of Jesus and our own.[304] To Kay, the eschatological cross-resurrection event is God's powerful breaking into the present age of evil through Christ to redeem and rescue people from it.[305] While Kay acknowledges the eschatological aspect of the Gospel, the Black Ecclesial Orthodox position would argue that the cross-resurrection event was primarily to free people from sin *and* it provides freedom from the "present evil age."

In this sense, the Gospel preached should lead to people find forgiveness and hope. Isaac Rufus Clark says the Word of God is "the content of the gospel being proclaimed—holy stuff being delivered to needy people for the purpose of feeding hungry souls the manna

---
[304] James F. Kay, *Preaching and Theology* (St. Louis, MO: Chalice Press, 2007), 27.
[305] Ibid., 34.

most satisfying."[306] The content of the Gospel is grace, which brings about forgiveness of sin and an enablement to live in fellowship with God. Repentance and alignment with Christ are the central goal of the Gospel in the Black Ecclesial Orthodox position.

The gospel content in the preaching moment also extends grace to the listening audience to grapple with the struggles of life and the damaging effects of sin. James Earl Massey argues that the Gospel is grace that meets the issue of human sin. He says, "real preaching is not merely concerned with the nature of religious experience; it helps the hearer to experience grace."[307] Grace, in his view, is when God allows us to grapple with the painful realities of a sinful and fallen world. In other words, the implications of the proclamation of Jesus's grappling with our sin and that of the world provide grace or help to the audience in the preaching moment.[308] This happens when the Gospel is applied to practical issues of life.

Some homileticians and theologians connected to the Black Church prefer to privilege the social implications of the Gospel over the individual. However, in the Black Ecclesial Orthodox Tradition, God is concerned with the whole person and society. Therefore, Gospel preaching is holistic. The Gospel first addresses concerns around individual righteousness and our relationship with God. Yet, it also addresses societal ills.

Vince Bantu in *Gospel Haymanot* says, "The 'good news' proclaimed in Scripture and encapsulated in the life, death, and resurrection of Jesus Christ is intricately tied to the kingdom of God."[309] He says, "The chief characteristic of God's Kingdom is that of *shalom*, the setting right of all things—personal and corporate." Therefore, in the

---

[306] Katie Geneva Cannon, *Teaching Preaching: Isaac Rufus Clark and Black Sacred Rhetoric* (New York, NY: Continuum, 2003), 46.
[307] James Earl Massey, *Designing the Sermon: Order and Movement in Preaching*, ed. William D. Thompson (Nashville, TN: Abingdon Press, 1980), 17.
[308] Ibid.
[309] Bantu, "An Introduction to Gospel Haymanot," 23.

preaching moments, one raises the call for repentance and forgiveness for personal sin through the sacrifice and resurrection of Jesus but, at the same time, can and must address issues of social injustice.

Bantu provides further rationale for this in discussing the Greek word *dikaiosune*. He rightly notes that "*dikaiosune* can be translated as either 'righteousness' or 'justice' depending on the context, and this concept can apply to personal moral integrity and social justice."[310] Therefore in preaching, when the Gospel calls people toward righteousness, fidelity to God through Jesus and personal morality is in view. This, however, does not diminish or deny the importance of justice; it demands Christians pursue it.

The Black preacher preaches in such a way that a nuanced and holistic hope is made visible. He or she is helping people to embrace hope for eternity because our sins are forgiven in the cross event. But also, the preacher is pointing to a living hope that comes from divine intentionality to face off against the realities of injustice. This reality of hope is foundational to Black Ecclesial Orthodox preaching. In *The Motif of Hope in African American Preaching During Slavery and the Post-Civil War Era*, Wayne Croft helps us see three complex expressions of hope in Black preaching during this period.[311] The first is otherworldly hope, where the emphasis is placed on eternal salvation or damnation. The second expression of hope focuses primarily on God's ability and desire to change a present situation. This expression would focus more on questions around injustice in the world. The third and final expression of hope is an apocalyptic hope that is more eschatological in nature. This type of hope looks to the end of time when God brings everything to a consummate point. However, proclaimed hope in the period of African enslavement and beyond was nuanced and multifaceted. It hung upon God and Jesus and was

---

[310] Ibid., 25
[311] Wayne E. Croft Sr., *The Motif of Hope in African American Preaching During Slavery and the Post-Civil War Era: There's A Bright Side Somewhere* (Lanham, MD: Lexington Books, 2017), 121.

comprehensive enough to address their present-day issues of injustice or suffering while granting hearers an eternal hope in Jesus Christ.

This is a hallmark of Black Ecclesial Orthodox preaching that has sustained Black people in America. We have maintained the tension of Jesus's death for our sins and his care for the suffering, primarily because we have always done theology and practiced it from the seat of oppression. Gardner Taylor argues that the proclamation of the Gospel "condemns and challenges and converts," and it speaks to fundamental issues of individual sin and the societal woes of racism.[312] The Gospel is holistic enough to address personal sin and societal evils.

The Preacher and the Pew

As I have stated earlier in this paper, preaching is the proclamation of the Word of God… through the agency of a preacher. This gives rise to another component of a theology of preaching: the role of the preacher and his or her relationship with the audience. In the Black Ecclesial Orthodox Tradition, the preacher is a herald or mediating agent of the Word of God in the preaching situation. It is the preacher's job to prayerfully mine Scripture to understand the text in the presence of God for the benefit of the people. The goal is to bring God's Word to life for that moment and to apply the Gospel to the listener's life.

In this sense, the preacher as the herald is what James Kay calls an "authorized messenger," who announces the destiny of Jesus Christ in relationship to ours. Kay says, "God has elected to convert humanity by means of humanity or determined that 'man is the medium' through which 'truth shall come to man,' then who are we to despise the human role accorded by God as intrinsic to divine revelation?"[313] God chooses humans as a mediating herald for the divine work of conversion in the preaching moment. Similarly, Isaac Rufus Clark says

---

[312] Taylor, *How Shall They Preach*, 86.
[313] Kay, *Preaching and Theology*, 130.

the preacher is the "proclaimer" of God's Word. Clark says of the preacher that we are "agents, stewards, representatives, and caretakers for the owner," who is God.[314] The preacher is, therefore, a "human agent" in the "divine preaching drama." The preacher is not the creator of God's message. Instead, he or she is the agent through which God speaks to the congregation in the present.

In Black preaching, rhetoric, or using available means of persuasion, is essential. As a heralding agent, the preacher is not passive in the preaching moment. Since the word is flowing through the preacher, the message certainly has the fingerprints of the preacher on it. While those like Richard Lischer believe preaching is solely theological,[315] it is in the work of the proclaimer that rhetoric plays a role in the enterprise of preaching. By rhetoric, I mean the work of the human relating the message to the people to move the congregation toward a God-faithful end. In preaching, rhetoric is employed in the way the Black preacher goes about storytelling; or in the use of word pictures, cadence, and tone of the preacher; and in the hopeful celebration. These are not tools for manipulation; they are used as a vehicle to carry the message forward.

Isaac Rufus Clark argues that rhetoric is necessary for Black preaching. Canon posits that rhetoric employed in preaching is "presenting logical evidence using the various techniques of argumentation, for preachers to bring to the mind of the hearers the 'presence' of matters that are of ultimate concern."[316] Clark's position implies that preachers must understand their audience to adequately address and move them toward action.

In Black preaching, the preacher seeks to identify with the audience by embodying the persona of a vicarious identifier. Gardner Taylor says, "He [the preacher] is not a mere emissary who is uninvolved

---

[314] Canon, *Teaching Preaching*, 44.
[315] Richard Lischer, "Why I Am Not Persuasive." *Homiletic*, 24.2 (1999), 14–17.
[316] Canon, *Teaching Preaching*, 17.

in the whole transaction of infidelity, guilt, and shame. On the contrary, the person who preaches is as guilty of the wrongs against God against which he inveighs as are those to whom he addresses his words."[317] Therefore, "A person's preaching is infinitely sweetened as he enters, actually or vicariously, into the plight and circumstance of human hope and heartbreak."[318] In this "vicarious experience, he is to bring the wounding and the healing of the Everlasting Evangel."[319] The preacher identifies with the plight and sin of the people and being a co-sufferer/co-sinner serves as a corrective for arrogant preaching and makes preaching more effective.

In the Black Ecclesial Orthodox Tradition, the preacher embodies this mediating role as an identifier because, in a real sense, the preacher understands sin and pain. After all, he or she is a sinner who is hurt too. He or she lives in the world and reads the same news about evils perpetrated upon people. Therefore, the preacher can understand the plight of the pew that needs mercy and grace because he or she needs it too. This identification means that in sermon preparation, the preacher is searching not only for what the congregation needs to hear but for what he or she needs to hear.

The Goal of Preaching

The final component of my theology of preaching has to do with the *telos* of preaching. From the perspective of the Black Ecclesial Orthodox Tradition, preaching is proclaiming God's Word from the scriptures to allow people to experience and hear God in the preaching moment (event),[320] to change lives (transformation), help people

---

[317] Taylor, *How Shall They Preach*, 29.
[318] Ibid., 34.
[319] Ibid., 35.
[320] Paul Scott Wilson, *Preaching and Homiletical Theory* (St. Louis, MO: Lucas Park Books, 2019) 60. See the above discussion around "preaching as event." This theory was developed from the Barthian idea that God is present in the preaching moment.

nurture a relationship with God, and instruct people on how to live in light of the scriptures.

Samuel DeWitt Proctor argued that the ultimate goal for preaching is a lasting relationship with God that plays out in how we live. Proctor says preaching should aim to "introduce and sustain… a relationship with God that enhances every dimension of life, and a discipleship to Jesus that provides a paradigm for the daily application and praxis of that relationship."[321] Thus, preaching addresses the God-human relationship and how it impacts our lives. The preacher aims for the congregation to look like and live like Jesus. Wilson says, "We use the term [transformation] to speak to what is effected through preaching; lives are transformed and conformed to the image of Christ."[322] That is, preaching is transformative and formative at the same time. In the preaching moment, God works through the Gospel as it is implemented through the Holy Spirit to reshape the lives of individuals into the likeness of Christ. It does so by providing the listeners with what is needed to live transformed lives. Bryan Chapell says, "the goal of preaching is not merely to impart information but to provide the means of transformation ordained by a sovereign God that will affect the lives and destinies of eternal souls committed to a preacher's spiritual care."[323]

Additionally, transformation helps the congregation to live like Jesus as witnesses in the world. Wilson argues for the corporate aspect of transformation. Citing Richard Lischer, Wilson argues that in the transformative element of preaching, the purpose of preaching is the moral transformation of the entire church into a caring community in the image of Christ.[324] Lischer says, "preaching, as opposed to

---

[321] Proctor, *The Certain Sound of the Trumpet*, 16.
[322] Wilson, *Preaching and Homiletical Theory*, 66.
[323] Bryan Chapell, *Christ-Centered Preaching: Redeeming the Expository Sermon*, Second edition (Grand Rapids, MI: Baker Academic, 2005), 25.
[324] Wilson, *Preaching and Homiletical Theory*, 66.

individual sermons, forms a community of faith over time."[325] In the Black Ecclesial Orthodox view, God uses preaching to change the congregation to look and live like Jesus so it can be a corporate witness in the world. A witness that proclaims the Gospel in word and lives out the Gospel implications of righteousness and justice in the world.

Conclusion

As I have stated previously, preaching is never done in a vacuum. Every preacher has theological assumptions that guide him or her through the process of preaching—from preparation to delivery of the sermon. In this work, I have attempted to insert what I understand to be some of the general theological assumptions of the Black preacher. Again, it is important to note that Black preaching is no monolith. This tradition is a vast body of water with many streams and tributaries pouring into it. Black preachers are shaped by different denominational influences, educational attainment, and theological distinctives. Yet, I believe there are some theological commitments that bring us to the same table. I hope that people from all backgrounds can drink from this living body of water. There is much to glean from the beauty of the Black preaching tradition, which communicates the Gospel that redeems people, brings hope, and challenges unjust systems with a unique and Godly vision.

---

[325] Richard Lischer, *A Theology of Preaching: The Dynamics of the Gospel*, Reprinted revised edition (Eugene, OR: Wipf and Stocks Publishers, 2001), **88.**

Beyond Racial Division: A Unifying Alternative to Colorblindness and Antiracism, George A Yancey, InterVarsity Press (ISBN: 978-1514001844), 224 pp., $15.49 (paper)

In his 2006 work *Beyond Racial Gridlock: Embracing Mutual Responsibility*, George Yancey addressed the intractability of racial conflict by addressing the inadequacy of various resolution strategies. In *Beyond Racial Division,* Yancey observes that little has changed and that the context for racial conflict has become even more charged. He offers again the model of *mutual accountability*, in which parties across racial dividing lines seek solutions to racial alienation that move processes forward. Mutual accountability through collaborative conversations seeks to address the concerns of both parties, settling for partial gains for both and solutions that can move both forward. He contrasts this with current practices of colorblindness and antiracism, which enter discussions with presuppositions and nonnegotiable stances that seek to impose restrictions on the other party. These all-or-nothing approaches leave no space for compromise, and as a result, there is no progress on the problems arising from racial alienation. This intractability undermines collaboration and movement for individuals and institutions alike. His appeal has compelling empirical and theological bases and should work based on these strengths. However, some concerns raise the question of effectiveness and the costs required for implementation.

My first question concerns the presentation of anti-racism as a failed strategy for resolving racial alienation. Essentially, do we need to define specific types of anti-racist practices that promote the *imago dei* of all persons by confronting institutional practices that privilege some representations of God's people over others? Shouldn't we discuss different types of anti-racism rather than lumping them generically with the worst examples of this strategy? I assume we are discussing institutional, systemic change rather than personal interchanges. It is hard to defend colorblindness as a personal or institutional practice, as both require denial of how social systems work and repudiation of the eschatological vision of Revelation 5:9 and 7:9. But we need a more nuanced engagement with what anti-racism *is* to do it justice.

As Yancey reports, leadership studies, sociological studies, and anecdotal accounts are replete with examples of poorly done anti-racism. These are often attempts to stake out platforms of power rather than transformative spaces where all can thrive interdependently. Moreover, it is no secret that institutional imposition of top-down, broad-based approaches without buy-in from the "rank and file" are doomed to fail. The irony is that many failed anti-racism or diversity efforts flout the principles Yancey has enumerated: forced compliance, flawed structures for engagement, no anchoring of objectives in institutional mission, and so forth.

However, if we are talking about Christian institutions, are we not beholden to biblical expectations to create a sense of belonging and to seek the welfare of all its members based on ethical commitments and biblical assumptions of the benefits for all in a body (1 Corinthians 12)? Often, this requires institutional postures where historically marginalized voices get to speak about what is lacking for mutual thriving. And if an institution operates out of a set of cultural norms that have not included marginalized voices, especially persons of color within the Body of Christ, then there must be conversations about change. Remember, persons from marginalized spaces *are already collaborating by choosing to be in said institutions,* so the onus is on the institution to take a posture that fulfills its mission and submits to a biblical imperative. Many organizations work out of this framework—for example, Edmondson and Brennan's *Faithful Anti-Racism: Moving Past Talk to Systemic Change* coming out of the Racial Justice and Unity Center or the Emmanuel Gospel Center's Race and Christian Community Initiative.

My second question concerns how one promotes buy-in for these collaborative conversations. Given the long historical arc of disappointment experienced by people of color in predominantly white Christian institutions, how will you obtain buy-in for the model? I have no doubt there is considerable incentive to improve conditions wrought by racial alienation. But the model, as it has been presented, makes assumptions about the preparedness of persons to participate. I speak here mostly of persons of color or, in a more generic sense, those social groups in a subordinate position in the social order. Yancey acknowledges the greater emotional and psychological burden subordinate groups must bear to participate in these conversations. It requires significant trust on their part to enter into these conversations, and right now, much of that is lacking. From a historical perspective, there are understandable reasons for this, and I will mention two.

First is the recent racial trauma suffered by many people of color over the past three years, signified especially by the deaths of George Floyd and others but also by other systemic assaults on their lives. Traumatized persons, especially those with generational trauma, have a very high trust threshold and will be understandably wary of entering into a process if they think it will not produce meaningful change.

Second, there is a long historical arc of repeated disappointment of people of color after taking a disproportionate emotional and psychological risk on promises made by those dominating the social order. In Christian contexts, this model is not something new. There have been various forms of "collaborative conversations" over the years, including, but not limited to, organizations like Promise Keepers, which made an explicit point of racial reconciliation as a goal, and multiracial church congregations. These examples, I would think, have an implicit commitment to this type of approach. But there has not been any staying power. Promise Keepers lost its impact after this explicit commitment, with active involvement in the organization diminishing considerably. In addition, sociologist Korie Edwards showed that multiracial congregations have rarely proved sustainable over time, often reverting to expressions of the dominant cultural paradigm or white folks leaving congregations, especially where there is Black or Brown leadership. Finally, of course, the overwhelming support of white evangelicals for Donald Trump in the 2016 election, a person who has a long track record of disdain for Black communities put paid to any remaining trust at that point. The message was clear to Christian communities of color: white believers would put their interests ahead of other believers of color when it was expedient. With such low existential trust levels, one might excuse the reluctance of folks of color to engage in another process where they have much more to lose if it fails.

Despite these concerns, I would recommend Yancey's work, especially for intentional communities where some level of trust across racial and ethnic lines has already been established. The groundwork of developing trust and addressing trauma will be essential. After that has been established, the disciplines of listening to the other and committing oneself to the common good, which Yancey advances, will have a greater chance of traction.

Nicholas Rowe
Gordon-Conwell Theological Seminary

8:46 Trumpet of Compassion: George Floyd's Last Breath and the Remaking of America, Tokunbo R. Adelekan, Day Rise Incorporated (ISBN: 979-8987234822), 448 pp., $24.58 (paper)

In *8:46 Trumpet of Compassion: George Floyd's Last Breath and the Remaking of America*, Adelekan draws the reader into the eye of America's cultural and socioeconomic storm of callous consumerism and cancerous commodification. In light of the rising political tensions and upheaval in response to rampant police brutality, Adelekan provides a timely ethical and spiritual analysis in order to lead citizens and scholars into the courageous charge of compassion—not simply emotional compassion but a Spirit-filled ethic of compassion and its transformative power to heal and reconcile. Following extensive exegesis of Scripture and American history, Adelekan defines transformative compassion as "the enlightened empathic energy that seeks the healing of the sufferer and the conversion of the enemy through life-giving and peaceful means. Transformative compassion goes beyond mere regard for the individual and contends that America can no longer live by the story of sacrificing the many to advance the powerful designs of an elite few" (p. 66). Though not new, this ideal is poignant to reassert for such a time as this.

Adelekan graciously invites us into this intimate and complex dialogue using the liberating, healing act of storytelling, also known as testimony. As he descriptively testifies of his personal experience of police brutality, he helps the reader identify why the murder of 46-year-old George Floyd on May 25, 2020, resonates so deeply in his soul. The 8 minutes and 46 seconds of time Minnesota police officer Derek Chauvin kneeled upon the back and neck of Mr. Floyd—causing death by asphyxiation, cruelly—fanned the flame to expose and renounce such apathetic and callous acts that stem from stony hearts. This scene becomes the launching pad for which Adelekan stakes his claim that an alarm like that of a holy trumpet must sound from on high; it must sound with the clarion call and resurgence of radical transformative compassion. Sacred compassion embodied by all will lead the charge of reconciliation in person and place. Adelekan uses significant stories within the Old Testament and fundamental tenets expressed by Jesus and Paul in the New Testament to undergird his framework before offering a couple of modern ministry expositional highlights as a scaffold for readers.

As a scholar and cultural critic with an extensive linguistic heritage, Adelekan uses excellent imagery and alliteration to convey his wisdom and methods of application. His vocabulary is expansive, and he wields his pen with such a poetic tenor that requires the reader (regardless of expertise, subject familiarity, or intellect) to double back and reread a sentence in order to grasp the layers of his points fully. As a true wordsmith, Adelekan writes with rhythm and invites the reader on an intentionally deepening dance through compassion's concept, components, context, and conscientiousness—compassion as emotion and ethic. He develops an argument that posits compassion as a holy emotion and ethic that we, God's people, are anointed to administer and must reclaim.

This book assumes the reader's high level of academic prowess and knowledge of scripture narrative. It is a theological composition placed within the context of recently publicized noncompassion acts, or what he calls "anti-compassion." As he thematically weaves current trauma, scriptural narrative, and Spirit-charged instruction, the reader is led to see a picturesque distinction between what transformative compassion involves and what anti-compassion reveals. I have compiled the list I have gleaned within the grid here:

Transformative compassion involves…		Anti-compassion reveals…
Listening	Upholding the values of human beings	Judgment
Access and vulnerability	Speaking in prophetic spaces	Self-righteousness
Willingness to suffer with	Prevention of moral suffocation	Stubbornness
Provision and problem-solving	Ujamaa	Disobedience
Development of Personal self-worth	Devotion	Apathy
Humanizing the enemy	Orientation toward other's predicament (Ujima)	Cowardice
Justice	Submission	Individualist-survival
Social reimagination	Sharing of one's gut	Othering
Faithful stubbornness	Entering the crude, ordinary reality of the other	Mentality of scarcity
Transparency	Reconciliation	Spiritual amnesia

Suffering is a concurrent theme within his analysis and a call to transformative compassion. Adelekan recognizes all too well the length to which an American cultural norm of hedonism has distorted the posture and experience of suffering. The honor he restores to the process of embracing suffering reminds me of Howard Thurman's expression of suffering as a spiritual discipline. He states, "as we suffer, God elects to suffer with them… God knows their sorrows. It is left for the people to know God's suffering" (pp. 52; 71). As Adelekan aims to reconcile suffering and compassion, we see the spiritual fruit in planting seeds of compassion as the sacrament of hope and communal reconciliation he proclaims. He posits, "Compassion highlights companionship, mutuality in the gift of burden-bearing. Suffering opens up the possibility of sharing and mutual growth, and by so doing, suffering is made meaningful. As we allow the Spirit to guide in our lifting of one another's burdens, healing occurs, birthing new life and giving rise to a vital community of hope in which evil is usurped and human potential flourishes" (pp. 110–111).

At the opening of "Part 2: Blessed Assurance," Adelekan states, "God wants a group of witnesses — people who see and experience Him — who then bear witness and represent Him to the world" (p. 82). He does well to highlight the witness of transformative compassion as it moves through the Old and New Testament narrative, conveying the premise that compassion is at the heart of God's covenant (p. 64). Adelekan then anchors the proposed ethic with modernized representation in two ministries, Pastor Robert Shipman, Sr. and The Prince of Peace Baptist Church and Dr. Elizabeth Conde-Frazier and the Esperanza Community in Philadelphia, PA. Using qualitative research methods of grounded theory and interviewing to gather the information for these excursus, Adelekan displays how compassion can be both critical and creative.

During a live "Conversation on Compassion" panel hosted by Palmer Theological Seminary and College, where Adelekan serves as faculty, another panelist and I asked: What witness do you hope your life will trumpet? What witness do you hope this work will help to develop in readers? To which he responded, "Hopefully, compassion can become a sacrament of hope!" He expressed that he aimed to tell a selective story of hope through the "spleen-gut formation" of compassion—a formation beyond mere theory that deep cuts to the core of our soul, which stirs humanity to activity as an expression of *metanoia* (life-change). He concludes, "The Christian teaching of compassion is not just a doctrine to be placed on a theological shelf, like too many doctrines, theological students are content to study merely. Christian history and world events demonstrate that practicing active compassion is a matter of life and death, both for individuals and for Christ's Church" (p. 83).

This witness and objective lead me to affirm the value of this book. I recommend this work to ministry leaders, seminarians, and justice-involved persons interested in using a restorative lens. No student in a seminary course on biblical or Christian ethics should go without exposure to the themes Adelekan has compiled within this book. Adelekan leaves us with a choice and an opportunity to partner with our Lord in the mission of Kingdom come through the timeless resuscitation of transformative compassion.

Lori E. Banfield
Eastern University

Race & Rhyme: Rereading the New Testament, Love Lazarus Sechrest, Eerdmans, (ISBN: 978-0802867131), 414 pp., $39.99 (paper)

African Americans, women, and other marginalized Bible readers often conclude that the Bible—both the Old and New Testaments—communicates that liberation is God's desire, even if that message has not always resounded loudly within mainstream Christianity. Yet, while we know that the Bible instigates and affirms our hunger and thirst for justice, we do not always agree regarding *how* the Bible affirms our liberation. This is to say that hermeneutical approaches differ even among marginalized people. A hermeneutic of suspicion leads some to reject the Bible altogether while, for others, it leads to deeper reflection. Sechrest performs the latter by exploring what sort of communication the Bible is meant to be and by also engaging "the ugly details in some biblical narratives" (p. 14). According to Sechrest, "A hermeneutic of suspicion helps us remember that uncritical appropriation of texts can do irreparable harm to the marginalized" (p. 15). Consequently, Sechrest employs "associative hermeneutics and womanist values" to develop what she describes as "a liberative hermeneutics of suspicion" (p. 13). Sechrest offers a thoughtful and practical guide toward interpreting the New Testament in a way that is life-affirming for those who have been marginalized, even in Christian contexts.

The first chapter, "Race and Associative Reasoning," could almost be a book of its own as it explains "associative hermeneutics," a process that demonstrates how even though the contexts of the ancient world and our world are different, our contemporary issues "rhyme" with topics treated in the ancient book called the New Testament. The first chapter also includes a comprehensive introduction to womanist hermeneutics. I imagine many instructors assigning all or parts of this first chapter just for the wealth of information regarding womanist interpretation.

Chapters 2 through 8 are treatments of several NT texts (in canonical order, mostly), attempting to demonstrate how those texts rhyme with contemporary issues related to race and racism. In each of these chapters, Sechrest not only interprets biblical texts, she engages with a variety of scholars—those within biblical studies as well as those in other disciplines who offer insights into racial dynamics in the U.S.

Chapter 2 ("Neighbors, Allies, Frenemies, and Foes in the Gospel of Matthew") is where Sechrest explores how Jesus relates to "the Other," shedding light on the relationship between victims of oppression and those from other communities who seek to be allies alongside those facing injustice.

Chapter 3 ("Assimilation and the Family of God in the Gospel of Luke") tackles the sensitive topic of how some racial minorities are accused of "acting white" when they engage with people outside of their own communities by treating the Jew-Gentile relationships in Luke's Gospel.

In Chapter 4 ("Sex, Crime, and Stereotypes in the Gospel of John"), Sechrest juxtaposes stories of some of the women in John's Gospel with those of contemporary women of color to turn the tables on how people were generally taught to read those stories. Current readers ought to see how women were victimized—sinned against rather than being the primary sinners.

Anyone claiming to value diversity—including those attempting to develop or participate in multiethnic churches—will do well to spend time in Chapter 5 ("Negotiating Culture in the Family of God in the Book of Acts"). Sechrest again examines Jew-Gentile relationships in Luke's writing to take up the issue of cultural compromise among diverse groups on the path toward Beloved Community.

Chapter 6 ("Privilege, Identity, and Status in 2 Corinthians") is a bold exploration of race, financial wealth, and social status for

Christians—especially leaders. Sechrest's discussion of privilege is especially engaging as she treats the various ways that privilege is conferred and wielded through her study of the Apostle Paul and his relationship with the Corinthian Christians.

Sechrest treats politics, law enforcement, and social movements—including public protests—in her exegesis of Ephesians. Chapter 7 ("Ligamental Leadership for the Household of God in Ephesians") touches on topics such as power, inclusivity, and leadership.

Chapter 8 ("Waking Up on the Wrong Side of Empire in Romans and Revelation") zeroes in on the Christian's relationship to the government—including policing. Sechrest does not hesitate to put a spotlight on the Trump administration and Trumpism, offering a prophetic word about how Christians ought to relate to Empire.

The book concludes with an appendix that consists of a classroom assignment (using Acts 4:1–22) designed to introduce students to the concept of associative hermeneutics. The exercise would be a helpful tool for groups to discuss Sechrest's hermeneutical approach with her entire book in view.

Since I was educated as a chemical engineer (and I believe Sechrest also has a science background), I appreciate ways of ordering and explaining things that I find to be logical. Consequently, I found *Race & Rhyme* to be logically organized with topics discussed thoroughly and illustrated clearly. I imagine fundamentalists and some evangelicals might not find Sechrest's project helpful, as she advocates for "taking the Bible seriously but not literally" (p. 16), even though many contemporary Bible readers who claim to read the Bible literally do not always do so. Sechrest's exegesis, however, relies on historical analysis of New Testament passages and pays close attention to the text. Sechrest is a scholar who has engaged topics related to race and Scripture in previous writings, and her expertise comes through in this book. As an educator, she writes with students in view—not just for other scholars in the guild—and each chapter feels like an invitation to explore associative hermeneutics even beyond the treated topics.

While there is no shortage of books on hermeneutics, *Race & Rhyme* is a rarity and is essential to New Testament studies in our time. It not only offers a framework for reading the New Testament generally, it also demonstrates how the New Testament can be read through a liberative lens.

Dennis Edwards
North Park Theological Seminary

Calling Out to Isis: The Enduring Nubian Presence at Philae, Solange Ashby, Gorgias Press, (ISBN: 978-1463207151), 350 pp., $75 (hardcover)

In the academic world, a person's first book is typically a revised version of their dissertation, and this study by Solange Ashby is no different. Yet, this study not only speaks to a scholarly audience but also an informed lay audience as well. This dual audience is one that is captured well in the choice of publisher since Gorgias Press is a reputable academic publisher interested in many different areas of the ancient world while also representing the keen interests of a lay readership focused on Eastern Christian studies and Oriental studies. It is worth mentioning that Ashby is the first African American woman to hold a Ph.D. in Egyptology, which helps the reader not only see the scholarly intervention that she is making in this study but also the European scholarly ground that she is trying to clear as it relates to the relationship between Nubia and Egypt in the ancient world.

The structure of this study is typical of a dissertation, as Ashby opens with an introduction followed by three main body chapters and then a conclusion. There are also helpful appendices that list out in more detail the different inscriptions from each period. The focus is on graffiti at a temple in Egypt and how particular identities can be formed by looking not only at the linguistics but also the social-cultural markers in the graffiti inscriptions. In this study, Ashby connects the different tribes that have been associated with the temple complex in Philae in Egypt and shows a unity between this group around the Isis cult. Ashby constructs this unity around the identity of a "Nubian"—that is, the people usually on the Nile beyond southern Egypt. Ashby provides a very brief background to the complex relationship that the Nubians have had with the Egyptians since the dawn of both civilizations, a scholarly conclusion that understands the term "Nubian" to be equated with non-Egyptian. Ashby brings this scholarly discussion into narrower focus as she examines the periods from the first century BCE and the fifth century CE. Ashby draws attention to the complexities of labeling the different worshipers at the Temple of Philae with a unified label because of the wide variety of kinship patterns by which these people would have identified themselves. Her intervention also draws attention to the problems that arise from labeling people because of the names that they use in the inscriptions. Ultimately, Ashby settles on the cultural subject matter to determine Nubian designation. Ashby's main thesis is that there was a Nubian presence at the temple in Philae from the first century BCE down to the fifth century CE, and while this presence took on different forms in the three phases that she marks, the temple marked an important religious and cultural marker for the Nubian peoples in Lower Nubia.

This thesis is worked out by looking at three distinct phases in the graffiti in Philae. The graffiti is in three different languages: Demotic, Meroitic, and Greek. Where most scholars have analyzed these separately, Ashby makes her analysis by taking in all three languages and hypothesizing the inscriptions in three different phases. In phase one (10 BCE–ca. 57 CE), Ashby demonstrates the battles waged among the Ptolemaic (Rome) Egyptians and the Nubians, ultimately resulting in Roman control over the temple at Philae and the Nubians being forced to pay the tribute for the temple cults. Ashby goes against previous scholarship to show that five of the inscriptions from this period were, in fact, Nubian because of the cultural and cultic material.

For the second phase (175–273 CE), Ashby draws the reader's attention to the plethora of inscriptions in this period, which highlights the change in power dynamics from Roman domination to Meroitic (one of the kingdoms of ancient Nubia) influence through the presence of a particular royal family and their involvement at the temple. Ashby notes the shift to priestly involvement for this family marks a shift in the broader cultural relationship between Nubians and this temple. A noted contribution from this section is the use of milk libations that are present in the graffiti and reliefs, which is something that other scholars have not noticed. Finally, in phase three (408–456 CE), Ashby explains again the shift in the power dynamics to another Nubian tribe, the Blemmyes, who lived more in the Eastern Desert compared to the river life of the Meroe. This shift was marked by nonliterate graffiti markings, which were made in worship to show that there were still rituals being observed in the temple by the new Nubian people. This study highlights the transitional period between the pagan Nile River Valley religions and the faith of Christianity that would soon absorb this region, resulting in the closing of this temple in the sixth century.

In the author's view, one of the biggest contributions of this book is the way in which it highlights the complexities around the term "Nubian," yet seeks to bring some unity through cultural identity in diverse language groups. While the issue of identifying the Nubian is complex, Ashby provides a unified approach not only with the evidence from the temple graffiti but also from other Nubian sites, which as she points out, is not very common due to subfield specializations in Egyptology as well as a lack of interest or familiarity with the broader field of Nubiology. As one of the long-standing enemies of the ancient Egyptians, the identification of the Nubian has been a preoccupation of many scholars throughout the 19th and 20th centuries. With many of the various groups from different times and places, it has been contentious to draw a conclusion as to who the Nubians were in antiquity. Ashby highlights this complexity but also tries to solve this anomaly during these periods by looking at how the different Nubians are interacting with the temple cults at Philae. She shows that while there may be Nubians, there are most certainly different kin groups that are more important to note.

This study could have been aided by the addition of a section highlighting the complexities of dating these temple inscriptions. Throughout the study, Ashby draws the reader's attention to the complexities of the dated material and what can and cannot be used within her analysis, but I think the reader would be aided greatly by a section that speaks directly to the complex nature of these dating schemes. Of course, this study is intended for scholars who are aware of the complex nature of these inscriptions, yet it would have been helpful to clarify for the reader, as she did with how the Nubians were being defined. That being said, for the student of ancient Christianity in Africa, these contributions will help give context to broader fields of scholarship like Egyptology and Nubiology, as well as highlight some useful pre-Christian cultural modes that the Nubians may have lived within, as well as cultural habits and rituals that may have entered into the later Nubian Church.

Mikail Berg
Brown University

A Multitude of All Peoples: Engaging Ancient Christianity's Global Identity, Vince L. Bantu, IVP Academic, (ISBN: 978-0830851072), 256 pp., $35.00

The West African philosophical idea *Sankofa,* roughly translated from the Akan language as "go back and take," is sometimes evoked without proper contextualization. Vince Bantu's historical account of ancient Christianity gives readers a deeper understanding of the Sankofa concept. The conventional narrative attributes the numerical growth of Christianity in the Global South since the previous century to the white missionary enterprise of the 15th century. Consequently, African Americans who reject Christianity condemn it for being a "Eurocentric, oppressive religion" (p. 4). In other words, it is the "white man's religion" (p. 6). Bantu argues that Christianity has always been global, and contrary to mainstream views, those in the non-Western world knew Christianity long before Europeans adopted it (pp. 1–6). This book complements several works with similar themes: Robert E. Hood's *Must God Remain Greek?: Afro Cultures and God-Talk,* Andrew F. Walls's *The Cross-Cultural Process in Christian History: Studies in the Transmission and Appropriation of Faith,* Thomas C. Oden's *How Africa Shaped the Christian Mind: Rediscovering the African Seedbed of Western Christianity,* and Jerome Gay, Jr.'s *The Whitewashing of Christianity: A Hidden Past, A Hurtful Present, and A Hopeful Future.* However, Bantu's book stands above these works because he didn't focus on one region; instead, he offered a survey of several territories with specific examples.

A Multitude of All Peoples is divided into four chapters. Chapter one deals with "The Roots of Western Christian Identity Politics." Bantu uses the biblical verses in Acts 2 as evidence of a diverse audience from different parts of the world at the time of the birth of the

Church (p. 9). Further, Bantu discusses how Christianity moved from its first-century roots—Palestinian Jews and the Aramaic-speaking community—to other parts of the world. Apostles such as Paul wrote the Gospel in Greek, the language of the majority population. In this way, Christianity was contextualized and disseminated far beyond its original boundaries (pp. 10–11). The growth of early Christianity was remarkable given the fact that the converts were persecuted as heretics (p.15). This situation changed dramatically when Emperor Constantine used Christianity to consolidate the Roman Empire (pp. 13–17). Additionally, even though Christianity was already present in Asia, the Middle East, and Africa, Constantine appointed himself as the "global patron," which created tension with Christians beyond the Roman Empire (pp. 18, 70). Although the rise of Islam weakened the spread of Christianity in Europe (pp. 51–71), Constantine planted the seed that Christianity is a Greco-Roman religion. This idea persists to the current times.

Chapter two surveys "The First Christians of Africa." Here, Bantu talks about Egypt as the gateway for Christianity into Africa through the missionary work of St. Mark (pp. 72–73) and how some of the earliest Christian manuscripts were found in Egypt (p. 73). Egypt was home to some of the most prolific Christian theologians and apologists (p. 74). The other African kingdoms that adopted Christianity before European missionaries were Ethiopia (p. 98), Nubia (pp. 84–95), Tunisia, Libya, and Algeria (p. 109). Christianity thrived on African soil, but the rise of Islam interrupted this process. Muslim jihadists imposed Islam in North Africa, which led to the decline of Christianity in this region (pp. 117–118).

In chapter three, we learn about "The Early Church in the Middle East" (p. 119). One of the daring actions taken by devotees in Syria was to write the New Testament in the Syriac language as opposed to Greek (p. 121). Bantu suggests that Syria has been dismissed and denied its rightful place in the history of ancient Christianity due to racial bias. In the seventh century, Christianity entered Lebanon

(p. 133). It was an important kingdom because it was here that Jesus performed miracles, such as turning water into wine. Ancient Christianity also gained a following in Arabia (p. 137), Armenia (p. 148), and Georgia (p. 159). What all of these regions shared is a devotion to the gospel, even in the face of strong opposition (p. 171). They also used the gospel to document and preserve their history (p. 154).

Chapter four chronicles Jewish Christians who imported their religion to Persia (p. 165). Christians from Asia were present on the day of Pentecost when Christ blessed his global church (pp. 165–66). Christianity also made its way to India (p. 180) and China (p. 205). Bantu's concluding recommendation is for his readers to understand that Christianity is a contextualized religion even though it is global.

The strengths of this book are the ample and compelling examples marshaled to uncover the Afro-Asiatic roots of Christianity. A limitation of this work is the minimal attention paid to pre-Christian religions. The peoples of Asia, Africa, and the Middle East had their indigenous religions that cannot be separated from their cultures and knowledge production. In this sense, Bantu contributes to the erasure of indigenous peoples' history, similar to Orthodox Muslim's view that whatever indigenous people were doing prior to Islam, it was *jahiliyyah* (Arabic for "ignorance"). Relatedly, the use of the word pagan (pp. 10, 17, 99) is problematic because there was no explanation or rationale for its usage. This is important because the term can be pejorative. Nonetheless, this book is a must-read. As my parents used to say, if you don't know your place of origin, you will aimlessly follow strangers. Bantu's work is a beacon for the aimless wanderers seeking clarity about the foundations of the ancient Christian Church. It is a lively rebuttal of the belief that Christianity is the white man's religion.

Yoknyam Dabale
Fuller Theological Seminary

www.ingramcontent.com/pod-product-compliance
Lightning Source LLC
Chambersburg PA
CBHW030553080526
44585CB00012B/369